FAITH, HOPE, & CHARITY

FAITH, HOPE, & CHARITY

A Modern Journey to God

CARDINAL RANIERO CANTALAMESSA

Published by Word on Fire, Elk Grove Village, IL 60007
© 2024 by Raniero Cantalamessa
Printed in the United States of America
All rights reserved

Cover design, typesetting, and interior art direction by Lily Fitzgibbons,
Clark Kenyon, and Nicolas Fredrickson

ISBN: 978-1-68578-118-7

Library of Congress Control Number: 2024931224

Contents

Part Three
I STAND AT THE DOOR AND KNOCK
The Gate of Charity

Introduction

NOVA
ET VETERA
(Mt 13:52)

THINGS BOTH
ANCIENT AND NEW

The pagans knew the myth of the "Three Graces"; we Christians know the three theological virtues: faith, hope, and charity. Three real, not mythical, graces! The name "graces" would be even more appropriate for them than that of "virtues," which is a category more philosophical than biblical and places emphasis on man's effort, rather than on the gift of God.

In Sandro Botticelli (1445–1510), whose painting is on the cover of this book, there is a clear spiritualization of the myth. The "Three Graces"—here unusually modest and chaste—invite us with their hands to look heavenward! Like them, the three theological virtues hold hands together because they are inseparable. Where one of them is present, there are also and necessarily the other two. It reminds us of the Trinity where, in each of the three divine persons, because of their common nature, there are also the other two. There is also a sort of *perichòresis*—that is, mutual interpenetration—between the three theological virtues, and it is interesting to know that the expression "the holy Triad" has been used to indicate faith, hope, and charity as well as the Holy Trinity.[1]

Taking advantage of the ancient tradition—both patristic and medieval—in this book, a modern and existential approach is also attempted; that is, one that responds to the challenges, enrichments, and, at times, surrogates proposed to the theological virtues of Christianity. The evangelical saying on the need to keep "the new and the old" together has been the chief guide of this essay, which has all the weaknesses (but, I hope, also some of the advantages) of any attempt at synthesis. No claim of completeness and systematicity, therefore, but only answers to questions and situations that are perennially relevant or that have become such with the advent of modernity. The division of the book into short chapters, which can be read almost independently of each other, responds to the approach that written communication has taken in the digital age.

The style and the liturgical framework adopted—a spiritual journey to Bethlehem in short daily stretches in the footsteps of the Magi—were dictated by the oral origin of the book, born as a development of the sermons delivered to the Pontifical Household, in the presence of Pope John Paul II in the Advent of 1992, and of Pope Francis in the Advent of 2022. The advantage of this approach is that it does not require us to spend all our time in defining what the theological virtues are, but it helps in getting down to the present-day reality and one's own life. The most important thing, in fact, is not to know what the theological virtues are, but rather to exercise them. We come to truly know them the same way we come to know Scripture: by practicing them!

Another advantage of this approach is that it helps to put theology within the reach of all the people of God and not just a few

1. In the quotation of sources, edition is only indicated for lesser-known writings or those not easy to find. The pontifical documents are cited from the Vatican website: http://www.vatican.va. "Man" stands for every human being in quotations from the Bible or past authors; "man" and "woman" are mentioned separately in every other context, according to the current standard.

"insiders"—a theology "capable of being preached," like the one advocated by Karl Barth and put into practice by St. Augustine. In fact, there is no content of faith, however high, that cannot be made comprehensible to every intelligence open to the truth. One thing we can learn from the Church Fathers is that you can be profound without being obscure. All that is required is to use a language accessible to all, which does not disdain images, stories, parables, poetry, and even modest personal experiences.

St. Gregory the Great says that Holy Scripture is "simple and profound, like a river in which, so to speak, lambs can walk and elephants can swim."[2] Our theology should be inspired by this model. Everyone should be able to find something useful in it, regardless of whether they are a beginner or an expert. Not to mention that it is often revealed to the "little ones" what remains hidden from "the wise and the learned"! (In order not to discourage anybody, some more specialized theological issues are treated in footnotes and in the two final excursus.)

At its core (developed in the third part, dedicated to charity), the present essay intends to be a timid attempt to do theology starting not from the philosophical idea of God as "absolute being" but from the biblical revelation of God as "absolute love." No foolish pretension whatsoever to substitute absolute love for absolute being, but rather a desire to fill an abstract and static *container* with a concrete and dynamic *content*. In other words, the need to give back to God the freedom of the wind, the ardor of the fire, and the pathos of a jealous lover that characterize him in the Hebrew Testament, as well as his paternal tenderness that only the Son who "is in the bosom of the Father" could reveal to us. What is attempted here has no other ambition than to entice others to continue it with better resources and more time before them! (A theme to be developed, closely linked to that of God as "absolute love," is that of God as "infinite humility.") A more

2. Gregory the Great, *Moralia in Job*, Epist. Missoria, 4 (PL 75, 515).

biblical approach does not mean giving up dialogue with modern culture; on the contrary, this essay, in its small way, wants to be a contribution to the evangelization of culture and to the enculturation of the Evangel.

Christian theology has not finished yet, I believe, with freeing the idea of God from the metaphysical cage of Aristotle and from the bandages of its own speculation that risk making God something like a mummy in the museum of the human mind! Aristotle's God moves the world without himself being moved, as the moon moves the tides; the Platonic "One," on the other hand, is Love (*Eros*) but, ignoring the Trinity, he has no one equal to him to love and be loved by, a bit like Adam before the creation of Eve. A joyless love and a wasted beauty!

What emerges in the end as the most beautiful (and for me unexpected) result of this undertaking is seeing the Christian dogma of the Trinity re-emerge in all its splendor as the solution of some never fully resolved theological knots. The revelation of the Trinity, we shall see, is what allows us to consistently say that God is Love, that he is Beauty, and that he is Happiness. The idea of making today's Christianity more palatable by putting the Trinity in brackets is like thinking you can make an athlete run faster by removing the spine from his body!

Plato and Aristotle, as well as their Christian counterparts, Augustine of Hippo and Thomas Aquinas, and all the great theologians of the past up to the present day, are the "giants" on whose shoulders we must stand to see further, even if only by an inch. When questioned, however, I am convinced that they would answer us just as inanimate creatures answered St. Augustine: "*Quaere super nos!*" (Search above us!). Above all of them there is Scripture, which—as the same St. Gregory the Great says—"grows with those who read it."[3] It grows also as new questions and challenges are put to it.

---

3. Ibid., 20, 1, 1: "[Scriptura] cum legentibus crescit"; Id., *Hom. In Ezechiel*, I, 7, 8.

A word, then, on the use of Scripture in this essay. To understand Scripture, is it sufficient to take into account the history of a text, the sources, the variants, and the literary genre—in a word, the most up-to-date exegetical criticism—or is something else also necessary? I think that all those means do not represent the last word, but rather a preliminary although indispensable one. Thinking that you can fully understand Scripture with the use of the most advanced scientific, historical, and philological techniques is like thinking that you can explain the Eucharist with a chemical analysis of the consecrated Host. And yet, no one is more ready to appreciate the critical work on the Bible (and is more grateful to those who dedicate their lives to it) than the one who uses it as a kind of "Instructions for Use" and as a springboard for the leap of faith.

An analogy can help us to see the problem. Scholars of the *Divine Comedy* of Dante Alighieri can go so far as to explain every word and discover every allusion and every historical or literary source of the text. Yet there will always remain something that escapes all of this and that is, however, the essential: that certain indefinable thing called poetry! This can only be grasped by the spirit of the reader, entering into tune and vibrating in unison with the spirit of the poet. Something similar happens with Scripture. "The Spirit testifies to our spirit" (Rom 8:16): this is the law that presides over every authentic reading of the Word of God, as long as it is done in communion with the Church, not individualistically and apart from Tradition.

The Bible cannot be read with the unspoken but sometimes evident assumption that it is the work of a human author, like any other religious book. There is a *historical* truth and a truth that we can call *real*, or *ontological*. Let us take Jesus' affirmation: "I am the way, the truth, and the life" (Jn 14:6). If, due to some unlikely new discovery, we would come to know that the sentence was in fact historically pronounced by the earthly Jesus, this would not prove it is true (the person who pronounced it could be deceiving himself!). What makes it "true" is that—in reality and beyond any historical contingency—he is the way, the truth, and the life.

In this deeper and more important sense, each and every statement that Jesus utters in John's Gospel is true, including his solemn declaration: "Before Abraham came to be, I AM" (Jn 8:58). "Truth" (*aletheia*) is almost synonymous with "reality" in the fourth Gospel! The classic definition of truth is "perfect correspondence between a thing and the idea of it" (*adaequatio rei et intellectus*); revealed truth is a perfect correspondence between a reality and the revealed word that expresses it (taking into account, of course, the context and the literary genre). The use of Scripture in this essay is inspired by these convictions. It has its model in the way Jesus, Paul, and the entire New Testament use the Scriptures. (Not always, though, in the way Church Fathers and medieval authors do!)

A remark also about biblical quotations. Translations of the Bible into modern languages are taking place nowadays at a pace of little more than ten years. Thanks to the progress of studies and changing linguistic tendencies (but also, in part, to justify their own existence!), translations continually change words and expressions that in the liturgy and in the life of the Church have been enriched, in the meantime, with harmonics that are lost. For this reason, while usually following the official translation of the American Catholic Church (NABRE), I allow myself, on some occasions, to use a translation or an adaptation that is more coherent, even grammatically, with the context of the discourse (as the Church does in its liturgy!), without resorting each time to the monotonous repetition of the initials "cf." or "see." (I suppose that every reader has a Bible available to verify if the quote is pertinent or not!) I shy away from an aseptic, mechanical, and almost chemical use of the Word of God. You cannot study the words of Scripture as you study fossils in sterile environments and with latex gloves. I fully agree with the following remark, which, though expressed by a poet, is no less valid theologically:

> Jesus did not give us dead words
> That we must close in small boxes
> And that we must keep in rancid oil . . .
> He gave us living words to feed . . .
> The words of life
> You can't keep them if not alive . . .
> We are called to nourish the word of the Son of God.
> It belongs to us, it depends on us
> To make it understood forever and ever,
> To make it resound.[4]

With joy and humility, in preparation for the second millenary of our Redemption in 2033, I offer this book on our common heritage to all fellow Christian believers—and to every person who in our modern society is longing for something "totally other."

Note to the present edition

What I have the honor and pleasure to present here to my English-speaking readers is a translation of the second revised and expanded Italian edition of the book released in 2024 by Edizioni San Paolo with the title *Fede, Speranza e Carità*. I express my deep gratitude to Dr. Liam Temple of Durham University, UK, for carefully reviewing, from a linguistic point of view, my own English translation, and to the editors of Word on Fire for the many intelligent suggestions.

The Author

---

4. Ch. Péguy, *Le porche du mystère de la deuxième vertu*, in *Œuvres poétiques complètes*, Paris, Gallimard, 1957, p. 587.

Biblical Abbreviations

HEBREW TESTAMENT

Amos	Am	1 Kings	1 Kgs
Baruch	Bar	2 Kings	2 Kgs
1 Chronicles	1 Chr	Lamentations	Lam
2 Chronicles	2 Chr	Leviticus	Lv
Daniel	Dn	1 Maccabees	1 Mc
Deuteronomy	Dt	2 Maccabees	2 Mc
Ecclesiastes	Eccl	Malachi	Mal
Esther	Est	Micah	Mi
Exodus	Ex	Nahum	Na
Ezra	Ezr	Nehemiah	Neh
Ezekiel	Ez	Numbers	Nm
Genesis	Gn	Obadiah	Ob
Habakkuk	Hb	Proverbs	Prv
Haggai	Hag	Psalm	Ps
Hosea	Hos	Ruth	Ru
Isaiah	Is	1 Samuel	1 Sm
Jeremiah	Jer	2 Samuel	2 Sm
Job	Jb	Sirach	Sir
Joel	Jl	Song of Songs	Sg
Jonah	Jon	Tobit	Tb
Joshua	Jos	Wisdom	Wis
Judges	Jgs	Zechariah	Zec
Judith	Jdt	Zephaniah	Zep

NEW TESTAMENT

Acts of the Apostles	Acts	Mark	Mk
Colossians	Col	Matthew	Mt
1 Corinthians	1 Cor	1 Peter	1 Pt
2 Corinthians	2 Cor	2 Peter	2 Pt
Ephesians	Eph	Philemon	Phlm
Galatians	Gal	Philippians	Phil
Hebrews	Heb	Revelation	Rv
James	Jas	Romans	Rom
John	Jn	1 Thessalonians	1 Thes
1 John	1 Jn	2 Thessalonians	2 Thes
2 John	2 Jn	1 Timothy	1 Tm
3 John	3 Jn	2 Timothy	2 Tm
Jude	Jude	Titus	Ti
Luke	Lk		

Part One

THOSE WHO BELIEVE IN HIS NAME

The Gate of Faith

1.
Lift Up Your Heads, O Gates!

There is a Psalm that has always had a great resonance in Christian prayer. It says:

> Lift up your heads, O gates;
> be lifted, you ancient portals,
> that the king of glory may enter.
> Who is this king of glory?
> The LORD, strong and mighty,
> the LORD, mighty in war. (Ps 24:7–8)

One hypothesis about the origin of this question-and-answer Psalm is that it refers to the moment when the ark of the covenant was brought to Jerusalem and placed in a temporary location, perhaps a pre-existing place of worship of a local divinity. The building had too narrow doors for the ark to pass through, so it was necessary to raise the front and widen the opening. The dialogue of the Psalm (recited, perhaps, on the anniversary of the event) would reproduce, in a liturgical and responsorial key, the exchange of words between those who accompanied the ark and those who were inside waiting for it. More simply, however, the Psalm could refer to the doors of the temple that open to welcome the God of Israel who, on solemn occasions, enters it with all his glory.

In the liturgy of the Church, the "doors" are those that open to welcome Jesus in his presentation in the Temple; or those of Hades at the Savior's descent into hell; or those of heaven that open to welcome the Risen One in his Ascension. In the spiritual interpretation of the Fathers, the gates spoken of in the Psalm are those of the human heart: "Blessed is the one at whose door Christ knocks," commented St. Ambrose. "Our door is faith. . . . If you want to lift up the gates of your faith, the king of glory will come to you."[1]

The door is not just an opening in the wall; it is a reality full of symbolic meanings. As a passage from outside to inside, it evokes hospitality, intimacy, and recollection. As a passage from inside to outside, it suggests liberation from prison, freedom, reaching out to others. Theological virtues realize both these symbolic meanings. They are doors through which God enters into us and through which we go out of ourselves toward God and our neighbor. The mystic significance of the door reaches its climax in the words the Risen One addresses to the Church:

> Behold, I stand at the door and knock.
> If anyone hears my voice and opens the door,
> [then] I will enter his house and dine with him,
> and he with me. (Rv 3:20)

The great door that we can open—or close—to Christ is one, and it is called freedom. "Freedom"—it has been written—"must move toward grace. Man is a besieged city and sin is the perfectly executed blockade. Grace is the king's army that comes to help. But man's freedom must make a sortie and go out to meet the liberating army. If the fortress does not receive help it is lost; but if it does not help itself through that sortie, it is equally lost."[2]

---

1. Ambrose of Milan, *Commentary on Psalm 118*, XII, 14.
2. Charles Péguy, *Note conjointe sur Bergson*, in *Œuvres en prose*, 2, Paris, Gallimard, 1961.

Freedom cannot precede grace; it would be heresy to think so; it must be open and eager to welcome grace. "Everything proceeds from God, but not leaving us as sleepy, reluctant to any effort and almost unwilling. . . . The one who created you without you, will not save you without you."[3] Advent is the liturgical sign of this mystery: we move to meet someone who is on his way toward us.

The unique door of freedom can be opened, however, in three different ways, or according to three different kinds of decisions, that we can consider as three distinct doors: faith, hope, and charity. These are doors that open from inside and outside at the same time: with two keys, one of which is in our hand, the other in the hand of God. We *cannot* open them without the help of God, and God *does not want* to open them without our cooperation. When a baby is born, its small lungs start functioning when they come into contact with the oxygen of the air. Without oxygen, the lungs would not be activated and it would mean death; but if the lungs are not activated it would be death all the same. This is what happens also in the relationship between grace and freedom.

Faith, hope, and charity are the three virtues most of God and, at the same time, most of ourselves. They are most of ourselves because in them our freedom is especially committed, and most of God because they are infused by him through the Holy Spirit, like germs that must blossom. This is how the *Catechism of the Catholic Church* defines them:

> The theological virtues relate directly to God. They dispose
> Christians to live in a relationship with the Holy Trinity. They
> have the One and Triune God for their origin, motive, and
> object. The theological virtues are the foundation of Christian
> moral activity; they animate it and give it its special character.
> They inform and give life to all the moral virtues. They are

3. Augustine, *Sermons*, 169, 11, 13.

5

infused by God into the souls of the faithful to make them capable of acting as his children and of meriting eternal life. They are the pledge of the presence and action of the Holy Spirit in the faculties of the human being. (*CCC*, §§1812–1813)

An Advent preface of our Italian Missal perfectly expresses the thought that the three theological virtues are the ways and doors to be opened to Christ who comes on Holy Christmas:

> Now he comes to us
> in every man and at every time,
> so that we welcome him in *faith*
> and testify in *love*
> the blessed *hope* of his kingdom.[4]

Faith, hope, and charity are the gold, frankincense, and myrrh that we, "wise men *coming from the West*," want to bring as a gift to God who comes to save us.

---

4. Advent Preface I/A.

2.

Jesus Christ, the Leader and Perfecter of Faith

Let's start our journey to Bethlehem with the first of the three theological virtues, faith. Faith is the great entrance door to the kingdom: "The kingdom of God is at hand. Repent, and believe in the gospel" (Mk 1:15). God—we read in the Acts of the Apostles—"had opened the door of faith to the Gentiles" (Acts 14:27). God opens the door of faith in that he gives the possibility of believing by sending those who preach the Good News; we open the door of faith by accepting God's offer.

With the coming of Christ, there is a leap in quality with regard to faith—not in its *nature* but in its *content*. Now it is no longer a question of a generic faith in God but of faith in Christ, who was born, died, and was risen for us. The Letter to the Hebrews gives a long list of believers—"By faith Abel . . . By faith Abraham . . . By faith Isaac . . . By faith Jacob . . . By faith Moses"—but concludes by saying: "Yet all these, though approved because of their faith, did not receive what had been promised" (Heb 11:39). What was missing? Jesus was missing, who—as the same letter says—is "the leader and perfecter of faith" (Heb 12:2).

The Christian faith does not only consist in believing that God "exists and rewards those who seek him" (Heb 11:6), it also consists in believing in the one whom God has sent. This is the

7

faith that Jesus means when he says: "Have faith in God and also have faith in me" (Jn 14:1). The great sin of which the Paraclete will convince the world is that it did not believe in him (Jn 16:9). When, before performing a miracle, Jesus asks "Do you believe?" and, after having accomplished it, he affirms "Your faith has saved you," he does not refer to a generic faith in God (this was taken for granted in every Israelite). Rather, he refers to faith in him and in the divine power granted to him. This is now the door of the "great faith," the faith that justifies the wicked (Rom 3:21–26), the faith that "conquers the world" (1 Jn 5:5).

For St. Paul, the saving faith has the Paschal Mystery of Christ as its specific object. It consists in believing that "Christ died for our sins and rose for our justification" (Rom 4:25). John, for his part, sees faith as embracing the whole mystery of the person of Christ, starting from his coming in the flesh. Speaking of the Word he says:

> To those who did accept him
> he gave power to become children of God,
> to those who believe in his name (Jn 1:12).

Accepting the Word means something more than just believing in his divinity, in what he is in himself. In the context of Christmas, faith, unfortunately, tends to be reduced solely to its ontological dimension—that is, to faith in the *being* of Christ, more than in his salvific *operation*. This is due to the heresies that marked and conditioned the reflection of the Church at the beginning—that is, Gnosticism, Docetism, Arianism, Monophysitism, and Nestorianism. All these heresies, in one way or another, pushed the Church to deal with the question: Who is Jesus? To what extent is he a man and to what extent is he God? Is he a human person or a divine person? The soteriological and kerygmatic content, by which Christmas points already to the Paschal Mystery, has remained somewhat in the shadows.

Significant, in this regard, is the different attention accorded to two verses of the prologue of John's Gospel: "To those who welcomed him he gave the power to become children of God" (v. 12) and "the Word became flesh" (v. 14). The first was as if relegated to the shadows by his more illustrious neighbor.[1] Yet this verse is no less important to the Evangelist than the other. Indeed, if becoming flesh represents the means, making men children of God through faith represents the end of the divine plan. "God became human"—the Fathers used to say—"so that humans would become divine."[2]

On this point, John is even bolder than Paul. He speaks of a true generation, of a birth from God; those who believed in Christ "were begotten of God" (Jn 1:13); in Baptism, we are born "from the Spirit," "reborn from above" (Jn 3:5–6); and believers in Christ are not just "called" children of God, but rather they truly are such (1 Jn 3:1). Paul uses the idea of adoption: "God sent his Son . . . so that we might receive adoption" (Gal 4:4–5); "He destined us for adoption to himself" (Eph 1:5). Human adoption, however, is simply a legal fact. The adopted child assumes the surname, citizenship, and residence of the adopting parents but does not share their blood and their DNA. For us it is not so. Not only does God transmit to us the name and rights of children but also his intimate life, the Holy Spirit, which, so to speak, is God's DNA in us. The difference between the two is only of language, though, because for Paul, too, it is the Holy Spirit who makes us children of God.

Christmas is the beginning of salvation, and as such, it already reveals its profound nature. It contains, albeit in embryo,

---

1. During the third century, the second of the two verses is cited 203 times, the first only 19 times. And the gap becomes much wider in the following centuries as the great Christological controversies develop.

2. Athanasius, *De Incarnatione*, 54.

the whole Good News of the Gospel. It says that in the fullness of time, God made his kingdom and his salvation come freely among us in the person of Jesus his Son. Like the five wise virgins, let us go out to meet the Bridegroom with the well-lit lamps of our faith.

3.
What Does Faith Give You?

Let us focus on the initial moment and the constitutive act of the theological virtue of faith, which is Baptism. The following short dialogue takes place at the back of the church between the minister and the candidate for baptism:

—Minister: "What do you ask of the Church of God?"
—Candidate (or parents): "Faith!"
—Minister: "What does faith give you?"
—Candidate (or parents): "Eternal life!"

The current Roman Ritual provides for the possibility of other responses equivalent to "Eternal life!"; for example, "The grace of Christ!" Suppose that the one to be baptized is an adult who comes to faith after a long journey in search for the truth, or of active atheism. To the question "What does faith give you?" I would suggest (and I would advise others to suggest) an even simpler answer: "God!" Faith gives you God!

There is an affirmation that only one person can make in the entire universe: "*I am God!*" (Is 45:22). On the lips of any other being it would be no less a blasphemy than that of Lucifer. Right below this affirmation, there is another that faith allows every human creature to pronounce: "*I have God!*" The difference between the Creator and the creature, thanks to faith, is reduced to what exists between *being* and *having*. God *is* God; the human creature *has* God! Faith makes God "my" God. How many times in the Bible do we hear this truth proclaimed: "O God, you are my God," and God, in turn, saying to Israel, "I will be your God and you shall be my people."

We will see later how these possessive adjectives are to be understood. For the moment, let us try to grasp what is paradoxical and breathtaking in all of this—namely, the happiness of not being God in order to have God. Think of a woman in love: she is happy not to be a man so that she can have a man; think of a man in love: he is happy not to be a woman so that he can have a woman. I am about to say something that sounds foolish. We humans are, in a certain sense, luckier than God! God does not have a God to love, to admire, and to share his joy with . . . we do. Soon, however, we discover that we are utterly wrong, because even God has a God to love, to admire, and to share his joy with. The Father has the Son, the Son has the Father, both have the Holy Spirit, and the Holy Spirit has both! What a stupendous mystery the Trinity! The reconciliation of everything takes place in it, even that of *being* and *having*, so difficult to achieve among us human beings.

Here, we see the tragic aspect hidden in atheism, especially in that form of atheism, or pantheism, which consists of putting oneself in the place of God and of making oneself God. Wanting to be God, one ends up not being God *and* not having him![1] It is so beautiful not to be God if that is the condition for having God! Even God would not be happy if he did not have a God to love and that is—as I have just said—if the Father did not have the Son, the Son did not have the Father, both didn't have the Holy

1. "We are God!" has sometimes been the slogan of the New Age movement. The suspicion that has always accompanied the so-called "mysticism of the divine essence" of Meister Eckhart and others is that the final goal of creatures is not the full possession of God but simply and purely becoming God, one being and one essence with him. The paradox of some Western followers of Pseudo-Dionysius the Areopagite is to linguistically exasperate God's transcendence while practically denying it with a pantheistic end-result. I think that "the infinite qualitative difference between the Creator and the creature" can never be totally abolished, not even in eternal life. This is not a limitation for us creatures, but the condition for the unending newness of our happiness.

Spirit, and the Holy Spirit did not have both. Each divine person finds in the other two his own complacency—that is, his own joy.

We Christians fully agree with the popular tale of the salt doll in Zen Buddhism; we just end it a little differently. The story tells us about a salt doll who wants to know what the sea is like. "To get to know me, touch me!" the sea says to her. She dips her hands in the water and her hands disappear; she dips her feet into the sea and finds herself without feet. The doll suffers and protests at losing part of herself, but when she is finally all melted, she jubilantly exclaims: "The sea, it's me!"

The "moral" that we Christians draw from the story is not "God, it's me!" but "God is mine!" The doll has discovered what the sea is; she has not discovered what water is and the "nature" of it! The sea is not *something* (nature, emptiness, nothingness, or whatever you want to call it); it is *Someone* who draws us to himself and who became flesh to be able to say to us what the sea says to the salt doll: "Touch me!"

But now we need to go back, as promised, to the meaning of the possessive pronouns "mine," "ours," and "yours." They can be taken in a "weak" sense and then they only mean that the creature "recognizes" God as the God in whom one believes. In the Bible, this first meaning is deepened, thanks to the concept of "covenant." The formula "I will be *your* God and you will be *my* people" not only indicates the relationship between God and the people but also the mutual belonging. For the Israelites, Yahweh is *their* God because he has united them to him in a formal covenant, and in every covenant, the resources of one side are shared by the other. This mutual belonging acquires a new dimension when the prophets begin to speak of the covenant in nuptial terms. "My lover belongs to me and I to him," says the bride of the Canticle (Sg 2:16). God is the bridegroom and his people are the bride. "On that day—oracle of the Lord—you shall call me 'my husband'" (Hos 2:16).

With the Incarnation, "that day" has become "today" (*hodie*); the marriage between God and humanity has been "consummated." They now belong to each other in a total and irreversible way: no longer as "betrothed" but as groom and bride. Jesus presents himself as the Bridegroom and his coming as the time in which the "King" celebrates the wedding banquet for his Son. The Apostle Paul (or whoever wrote the Letter to the Ephesians reproducing and developing his thoughts) presents Christ and the Church as the symbol and model of every human marriage. We can repeat in a much stronger sense the words of the Psalm: "O God, you are *my* God" because faith makes us children of God and children possess their own father; nothing and no one belongs to them more than he does. We should remember this when we say "*Our* Father."

There is more to this mystery but let us postpone further consequences until we talk about the third theological virtue, charity. There we will see to what extent, through faith, hope, and charity, God becomes "ours," his holiness becomes ours, and his Trinitarian love becomes ours. Yes, God is ours and we are his. With one difference, though: we belong to him *by right* (since he created and redeemed us), he belongs to us *by grace*!

4.
Is There Salvation Outside Faith in Christ?

If faith that saves is faith in Christ, what shall we think of all those who have no chance of believing in him? Are they excluded from eternal salvation from the start? Apart from the different ways of understanding the reality of the Church, all Christians shared in the past the traditional axiom from St. Cyprian: "Outside the Church there is no salvation."[1] Following the divisions between Christians, the circle was further narrowed and the saying was used to affirm that outside "one's own" Church (Catholic, Orthodox, Evangelical, etc.), there is no salvation.

Today, this is no longer the case, unless we understand "Church" in the broad sense of the Augustinian *Ecclesia ab Abel,* which embraces all the righteous who lived from Abel onward.[2] That axiom, moreover, has never been a dogma or an article of the Credo, but only a shared theological conviction. Originally, it had a local and particular meaning, not a universal one. It meant that those who have known Christ and do not accept the Church cannot be saved. It applied to those for whom it was directly intended—that is, local heretics and schismatics between Carthage and Rome—certainly not to populations whose existence was not even known, such as those in the Americas or the Far East.

---

1. "Extra Ecclesiam nulla salus": the statement goes back to St. Cyprian, who repeats it in some of his writings. The formulation, closest to that which has become traditional, is in the *Letter 4 to Pomponius* (4.3): "Nemini salus esse nisi in ecclesia [potest]."

2. Augustine, *Comm. on the Psalms*, 118, 20, 1 and 27, 2.

For some time, there has been a dialogue among religions based on mutual respect and recognition of the values present in each of them. In the Catholic Church, the starting point was the declaration *Nostra Aetate* of the Second Vatican Council, but a similar orientation is also shared by the other historical Christian Churches. With this recognition, the conviction has gained ground that even people outside the Christian Churches can be saved.

Is it possible, in this new perspective, to maintain the role once attributed to "explicit" faith in Christ? In this case, would not the ancient axiom "Outside the Christian Church there is no salvation" survive in the variant "Outside *Christian faith* there is no salvation"? In this way, however, salvation is limited from the start to a tiny minority. Can we be at ease with this conclusion and, above all, does it not offend Jesus by cutting him off from a large part of humanity? We cannot believe that Jesus is God, that he is the greatest gift of God the Father to the world, and then restrain his relevance to a very limited sector of humanity that had the privilege of being born in a Christian country. Jesus is "the savior of the world" (Jn 4:42) and the Father sent the Son "that the world may be saved through him" (Jn 3:17): the world, not a few people of the world! "God wills everyone to be saved and to come to knowledge of the truth" (1 Tm 2:4).

In John's Gospel, Jesus says: "I have other sheep that do not belong to this fold. These also I must lead, and they will hear my voice, and there will be one flock, one shepherd" (Jn 10:16). In the past, these words were understood to mean that the "one flock" was one's own particular Church and the "one shepherd" was the supreme head of it (for us Catholics, the pope!). But for Jesus (and for John who relays his words), the only flock is the one formed not only by Jews but also by Gentiles, and "the only shepherd" is Christ himself.

"God does not deny his grace to anyone who does all that

is within him."[3] This axiom has run through the entire history of theology from the Church Fathers onward, but has ended up being applied, in a very restricted sense, to the debate on justification by faith. Once freed from all the technical and polemical meanings with which it has been overloaded ("For himself, man can do absolutely nothing to save himself!"), this axiom can be a good starting point for interreligious dialogue.

Scripture teaches us that those who do not know Christ but act on the basis of their conscience (Rom 2:14–15) and do good to their neighbor (Mt 25:31–40) are acceptable to God. In the Acts of the Apostles, we hear, from the mouth of Peter, this solemn declaration: "In truth, I see that God shows no partiality. Rather, in every nation whoever fears him and acts uprightly is acceptable to him" (Acts 10:34–35).

In that age, the "acceptance" of God referred to the "devout" Gentiles who sympathized with the Jewish religion, but in today's broader horizon, his statement should be extended to every human person. Even adherents to other religions generally believe that "God exists and rewards those who seek him" (Heb 11:6). Therefore, they realize what Scripture considers the fundamental and common datum of all faith. This applies in particular to the Jewish brothers who believe in the same God of Abraham, Isaac, and Jacob in whom we Christians believe.

The main reason for our optimism is not based, however, on the good that adherents to other religions are able to do but on the "multiform grace of God" (1 Pt 4:11). God has far more ways to save than we can think of. It is true that he has instituted "channels" of his grace, but he has not bound himself to them. "The Holy Spirit"—says a text from Vatican II—"in a way known to God, offers every person the possibility of being associated with the Paschal Mystery" (*Gaudium et Spes*, 22). Sometimes I feel the need to offer the sacrifice of the Mass precisely in the name of all

---

3. "Facienti quod in se est, Deus non denegat gratiam."

those who are saved by the merits of Christ but do not know it. The liturgy also urges us to do so. In Eucharistic Prayer IV, in the intercession for the pope, the bishop, and the faithful, a prayer is added "for all who seek you with a sincere heart."

One of the "extraordinary" means of salvation is suffering. After Christ has taken it upon himself and has filled it with his presence, pain is also, in some way, a universal sacrament of salvation. Every suffering—not just that of believers—mysteriously accomplishes, in some way, "what is lacking in the passion of Christ" (Col 1:24). The Church celebrates the Feast of the Holy Innocents, yet they did not know they were suffering for Christ!

We know that all those who are saved are saved by the merits of Christ: "There is no salvation through anyone else, nor is there any other name under heaven given to the human race by which we are to be saved" (Acts 4:12). "No one comes to the Father except through me" (Jn 14:6)—there are no exceptions to this rule. However, it is one thing to affirm the universal need of *Christ* for salvation and another thing to affirm the universal necessity of *faith in Christ* for salvation. We should avoid falling back into the error we want to combat—that is, of making salvation and grace depend on human contribution, reducing faith itself to a "work."

Is it superfluous, then, to continue proclaiming the Gospel to every creature? Far from it! It is the intention that must change, not the fact. We must continue to proclaim Christ, not so much for a negative reason—otherwise the world will be condemned—as for a positive reason: because of the infinite gift that Jesus represents for every human being. Christ's mandate "Go into the whole world and proclaim the gospel to every creature" (Mk 16:15) and "Make disciples of all nations" (Mt 28:19) retains its perennial validity, but it must be understood in its historical context. His words refer to the time they were written. At that moment, "the whole world" and "all peoples" was a way of saying that Jesus' message was not intended only for Israel but also for the rest of the world. They are always valid for everyone, but for those who already belong to a religion, it takes respect, patience, and love. To his friars who went "among the Saracens," Francis of Assisi gave instructions that are still valid today:

> The brothers who go among the Saracens may conduct themselves in two ways spiritually among them. One way is not to make disputes or contentions; but let them be *subject to every human creature for God's sake*, yet confessing themselves to be Christians. The other way is that when they see it is pleasing to God, they announce the Word of God, that they may believe in Almighty God—Father, and Son, and Holy Ghost, the Creator of all, our Lord the Redeemer and Savior the Son, and that they should be baptized and be made Christians.[4]

What should worry us most is not the fate of those who did not know Christ; it is that of those who knew him but "ignored" him. Addressing the cities of Galilee that had not accepted his message, Jesus says that the fate of the pagans on the Day of Judgment would be better than that of unbelieving Israel: "Woe to you, Capernaum; woe to you Bethsaida" (Mt 11:20–24). A salutary warning for us Christians!

---

4. *Rule without a Bull*, chap. XVI.

5.
Faith and the Sense of the Holy

In order to approach God—we read in the Letter to the Hebrews—one must first of all "believe that he exists" (Heb 11:6). Even before, however, believing that he exists—which is already having approached—it is necessary to have at least a certain hint of his existence. A famous theologian of the past calls it "a sense and a taste of the infinite,"[1] and a later writer, "the sentiment of something oceanic."[2] This is what Rudolph Otto has called the sense of the holy, "the numinous," and the "tremendous and fascinating mystery."[3] St. Augustine surprisingly anticipated this discovery of modern phenomenology of religion. Turning to God, in his *Confessions*, he says: "When I met you for the first time . . . I trembled with love and horror."[4] And again: "I shiver and I burn; I shiver because of the distance, I burn because of the resemblance."[5] It is a feeling often accompanied by a shiver that makes one get goosebumps. Ghost stories and horror films are modern, secularized ways of experiencing this feeling.

If the sense of the sacred has fallen in the modern technological world, nostalgia for it remains. Someone has defined it, in

---

1. Friedrich Schleiermacher.
2. Romain Rolland.
3. Rudolph Otto, *Das Heilige*, 1917 (*The Idea of the Holy*).
4. Augustine, *Confessions*, VII, 10: "contremui amore et horrore."
5. Ibid., XI, 9: "et inhorresco et inardesco."

secular terms, as "longing for the totally Other."[6] Young people, more than others, feel the need to be carried away from the banality of everyday life and to "escape." Those who attended famous rock concerts (e.g., the Beatles, Elvis Presley, Woodstock Festival of 1969) and who take part today in mega-gatherings of singers and bands are transported away from their everyday world. They are projected into a higher dimension that gives the impression of something transcendent and sacred. The experience of vibrating in unison with a multitude enormously amplifies the emotion of the individual. The term "fan" (abbreviation of fanatic) is the secularized equivalent of "devotee," and the qualification of "idols" given to their favorites has a clear religious resonance.

These mass gatherings can have their artistic value and sometimes convey noble and positive messages, such as peace and love. They are "liturgies" in the original and profane sense of the term—that is, shows offered to the public out of duty or to obtain their favor. They are not, of course, the only or the best opportunities for an experience of the "totally other," not even for young people. For someone it can be the first smile of one's child, witnessing an awe-inspiring natural phenomenon or panorama,[7] listening to a sublime piece of music, or contemplating a masterpiece of art. Two things had such power for the philosopher Kant: the starry sky above him and the moral conscience within him.

Let us try to perceive how the Church can be, for people of today, the privileged place for an experience of the true "totally other," which is God. The most common occasion is the liturgy. The Catholic liturgy has passed, in a short time, from being an action with a strong sacred and priestly imprint to a more communitarian and participatory action, where all the people of God have their part, each with their own ministry.

At the beginning of the Church and for the first three

---

6. Max Horkheimer, *Die Sehnsucht nach dem ganz Anderen*, 1972.

7. From an experience of this kind, the beautiful hymn "How Great Thou Art" of the Swedish poet Carl Gustav Boberg (1859–1940) was born.

centuries, the liturgy was truly a "liturgy"—that is, the action of the people (*laos*, people, is among the etymological components of *leitourgia*). From St. Justin, the *Traditio Apostolica* of St. Hippolytus, and other sources of the time, we obtain a vision of the Mass that is certainly closer to the reformed one of today than to that of the centuries behind us. What happened after then? The answer is an awkward word that we cannot avoid: clericalization! In no other sphere has it acted more conspicuously than in the liturgy.

Christian worship, and especially the Eucharistic sacrifice, both in the East and in the West, underwent a rapid transformation from being an action of the people to being an action of the clergy. For centuries, the central part of the Mass, the Canon, was pronounced by the priest in Latin, in a low voice, from behind a curtain or a wall (a temple within the temple!), out of the sight and the hearing of the people. The only contact of the laity with the Eucharist was the visual one at the elevation of the Host. There is an evident return to what happened in the worship of the first covenant when the High Priest entered the *Sancta sanctorum*, with incense and the blood of the victims, and the people stood outside trembling, overwhelmed by the sense of God's tremendous holiness and majesty.

The sense of the sacred is at its highest here, but, after Christ, is it the right and genuine one, complete in all its components? This is the crucial question. The New Testament is very explicit on this point. In the Letter to the Hebrews we read:

> You have not approached . . . a blazing fire and gloomy darkness and storm and a trumpet blast and a voice speaking words such that those who heard begged that no message be further addressed to them. . . . No, you have approached . . . Jesus, the mediator of a new covenant, and the sprinkled blood that speaks more eloquently than that of Abel. (Heb 12:18–24)

The sacred has changed its way of manifesting itself: no longer so much as a mystery of majesty and power but as a mystery of infinite proximity and accessibility. "Through the blood of Jesus we have confidence of entrance into the sanctuary by the new and living way he opened for us through the veil, that is, his flesh" (Heb 10:19–20).

We must be careful, however, not to stress the contrast too much. To do so would mean misunderstanding the novelty brought by Christ regarding the sentiment of the holy. First of all, the image of a good, merciful, and even tender God is far from absent or marginal in the Hebrew Testament; on the other hand, in the Gospel, God does not cease being "Lord of heaven and earth" (Mt 11:25). The real novelty is that God, remaining what he is—i.e., Almighty, Transcendent, and Holy—is now given to us as a father! And no longer just a father in a metaphorical sense, as he was before Christ, but as a true and "natural" father, since we have become sons in the Son, "participants in the divine nature" (2 Pt 1:4).

Jesus enclosed this novelty in the initial invocation of the prayer that he left us. God is "*Our Father*"—that is, a very tender father (*abba*!) to whom we can address ourselves with the same freedom and confidence as a child to his or her dad; but he is "*in heaven*,"—that is, as above us as heaven is above the earth. The Church has gathered this same image of God in the initial words of the creed: "I believe in God the Father almighty": Father, but almighty; almighty, but Father! After all, is this not what children unconsciously expect from their earthly father—namely, that he be tender and accessible but also strong and authoritative to protect them in life?

6.
Believing Is to Obey

Traditional theology distinguishes between two types of faith: objective faith, which indicates the truths to be believed, and subjective faith, which indicates the very act of believing. We can call the first *believed* faith and the second *believing* faith—that is, faith with which one believes.[1] We mean the first kind of faith when we speak of the faith "transmitted to believers once and for all" (Jude 3), of the "deposit of faith," and the "truths of faith." We mean the second in the words "Increase our faith" and "If you had faith as much as a mustard seed" (Lk 17:6).

Believed faith engages the intellect above all and consists in assenting to revealed truths. Believing faith engages the will first of all and consists in a confident abandonment of the whole being to God. The first consists in believing *something*, the second in believing in *someone*.

Of the two dimensions of faith, the objective and the subjective dimension (but also, we shall see, of the other two theological virtues), ancient and Scholastic thought has privileged the first—that is, what they are in themselves, their object and their mutual relations. All the treatises *On faith* (*De fide*) of the patristic era deal with the content of faith and its orthodoxy. St. Augustine, who wrote the first treatise (he calls it a manual, *enchiridion*) on the three theological virtues, says that the discourse

---

1. According to the theological language: *fides quae* (*creditur*) and *fides qua* (*creditur*).

on them consists in knowing "what to believe, what to hope for, what to love."[2]

Modern thought, on the other hand, highlights the second component of the theological virtues—i.e., their existential dimension, including how they operate in those who receive them. Simplifying things (maybe excessively), we could say: the ancients ask themselves what to believe, what to hope for, and what to love; the moderns, what *it is* to believe, what *it is* to hope, what *it is* to love. Existential faith does not limit itself to making us believe that Jesus has risen and is alive: it makes us *feel* that! It is always accompanied by a motion and an anointing of the Holy Spirit (1 Jn 2:27).

It would be contrary to the law of the "homogeneous development of tradition" to contrast these two approaches or to choose between them. The "new things" must be added, not substituted for the "old things." These are the base, those are the exponent: the base can be without the exponent, but the exponent cannot be without the base![3]

The *believed faith*, or the content of the faith, is summarized in the symbol of faith—that is, the creed of the Church—and even more succinctly in the formulation the *Catechism* gives of the two main mysteries of faith: the unity and trinity of God, and the Incarnation, Passion, Death, and Resurrection of our Lord Jesus Christ.

We cannot do the same with the other dimension of faith, the *believing faith*. It consists in fact of a unitary interior attitude and is placed at the end of a process of which St. Paul, in Romans 10, traces the various phases, drawing them, so to speak, on the map of the human body.

2. Augustine, *Enchiridion*, I, 3 e I, 6 (PL 40, 232–233): *Quid credendum, quid sperandum, quid amandum.*

3. If there is a criticism I would make of Søren Kierkegaard, the philosopher I am most indebted to in this essay, it is precisely that of stressing the contrast between objectivity and subjectivity to the point of making them seem incompatible. Another gap is the very limited importance assigned to the Trinity in his thinking.

25

Everything begins, he says, from the ears—that is, from hearing the proclamation of the Gospel: "faith comes from listening" (*fides ex auditu*). From the ears, the movement passes to the heart, where the fundamental decision is made: "with the heart one believes" (*corde creditur*). From the heart, the movement goes up to the mouth: "with the mouth one makes the profession of faith" (*ore fit confessio*).

The process does not end here. From the ears, the heart, and the mouth, it passes to the hands because "faith becomes *operative* in charity" (*fides per caritatem operatur*) (Gal 5:6). We are not justified *because* of our works but neither are we saved *without* our good works! The just requirement of St. James is satisfied: there is also room for the "works"! Not as a condition for but as a consequence of being justified. At this point, however, the discourse passes from the first to the third theological virtue, charity, and we will postpone it to the moment when we return to it later.

Let us go back for a while to St. Paul's "map": ears, heart, mouth, hands. One of these stages deserves a special attention: that of the heart. Some of Blaise Pascal's most famous *Thoughts* are the following: "The heart has its reasons that reason does not know. . . . The heart, and not the reason, feels God. This is what faith is: God felt by the heart and not by reason."[4] This is indeed a bold statement, but one that has the highest authority behind it. The Apostle Paul knows and often uses the word *nous*, which corresponds to the modern concept of mind, intelligence, or reason; but he does not say *mente creditur*, "with the mind one believes"; he says—we have heard—*corde creditur* (*kardia gar pisteùetai*), "One believes with the heart." God is "felt by the heart and not by reason," as Pascal says, for the simple fact that "God is love," and love is not perceived with the intellect but with the heart.

Unfortunately, it is not Pascal's "reasons of the heart" that have shaped the secular and theological thinking of the last three

4. Blaise Pascal, *Pensées*, 277–278, ed. Brunschvicg.

centuries, but rather the *Cogito ergo sum* (I think, therefore I exist) of his compatriot Descartes, even if against the intention of the latter, who always remained a pious Christian and a believer. (His name is on the list of famous pilgrims to the Marian shrine of Loreto—November 10, 1619).

The consequence was that rationalism dominated and dictated the law before arriving at the current nihilism. All the speeches and debates that take place, even today, focus on "faith and reason," never, as far as I know, on "faith and the heart" or "faith and the will." In another of his thoughts, Pascal says that faith is clear enough for those who want to believe, and dark enough for those who do not want to believe.[5] Believing, in other terms, is a disposition of the will before being a question of reason and intellect.

We ask ourselves: What is the final act of the process that leads to faith in Christ? What is the answer that God expects from a human being? John, as we have already seen, sums it up in one word: "welcome." To those who welcomed him, believing in his name, he gave the power to become children of God. Throughout the entire fourth Gospel, everything is decided by whether Christ and his testimony are accepted. People are divided into two categories: those who accepted him and those who did not accept him; those who have opened their eyes to the light and those who have closed them. Hence the close connection in John between *believing* and *knowing* (Jn 6:69; 1 Jn 4:16).

Paul, too, has a word with which he summarizes his idea of faith. It is certainly not alternative to that of John but highlights an essential component of it: faith is *obedience* (Rom 1:5, 16:26). A very particular obedience, indeed, different from what we usually mean by this word! It is a confident abandonment, an unreserved surrender—soul and body, for life and death—to Christ and, through him, to God the Father in the Holy Spirit.

5. Ibid., 430, ed. Br.

Something no human authority can claim. This attitude finds its highest expression in the moment in which a person, in the amazement of a nascent (or re-nascent!) faith, exclaims: "Jesus is Lord!" (Rom 10:9).

What is so special about this exclamation that makes it the gateway to salvation and that nobody can utter it "without the Holy Spirit" (1 Cor 12:3)? The first, objective reason is that the whole Paschal Mystery of Christ is summarized in it. In fact, "for this reason Christ died and returned to life: to be the Lord of the dead and the living" (Rom 14:9). The second, subjective reason is that by saying "Jesus is Lord!" not only is a fact affirmed but a decision is also made. It is like saying: "Jesus is *my* Lord; I submit to him; everything about me belongs to him; he has all rights over me, having ransomed me at a high price."

All of this should be said with joy and freedom because there is no greater happiness for people in love than belonging to the loved one and no longer to oneself. *Believing faith* is a nuptial "Yes!" pronounced on the altar of one's heart.

7.

But Not Everyone Obeyed the Gospel!

The Apostle Paul develops the description of the process that leads to faith in the same chapter in which he deals with his fellow Jews' refusal to believe: "But not everyone obeyed the Gospel" (Rom 10:3). This obliges him to speak also of the opposite outcome of the process, that of the refusal to obey the Gospel and to believe in Christ. Since, as we will see, this concerns us Christians no less than the Jews of that time, it is necessary that we also reflect on it. The Apostle writes of his compatriots: "In their unawareness of the righteousness that comes from God and their attempt to establish their own [righteousness], they did not submit to the righteousness of God" (Rom 10:3).

Reading these words, an image comes to my mind, almost a parable. If it were Jesus who narrated it, I think it would sound more or less like this:

> A man was weaving a piece of rough cloth in his loom. He wanted to make a new suit with which to present himself to the king who had invited him to a wedding feast. One day someone knocked at his door. The visitor came from the king in person and carried, carefully resting on his two arms, a splendid outfit of purple and fine linen to wear at the royal banquet. The man thought to himself: "How will I repay? What will they ask me to do in return?" He, therefore, sent

word to the king that he should not have concerned himself so much and that, after all, he had almost finished weaving his own suit. Having sent the messenger back, he returned to the basement to weave his rough cloth suit. How did he regret that later! When the day came and he went to the king's palace, he was rejected at the door for he was not wearing the wedding garment.

This parable had its first draft in the Bible. Isaiah speaks of two clothes: one woven by us with "our acts of righteousness" (Is 64:5) that resembles an "unclean cloth" and another, received from God, of which it is said: "He has clothed me with the garments of salvation; he has wrapped me with the mantle of righteousness" (Is 61:10). The Jews of the time of Christ—the Apostle remarks with sadness—chose the first way. They wanted to weave their own clothing with the works of the law. But the Apostle knows that the risk did not end with the Pharisees of that time. The choice is also before Christians, and the outcome is always uncertain. This is why St. Paul writes his letters to the Galatians and to the Romans. In the first, he exclaims: "O stupid Galatians! . . . I want to learn only this from you: did you receive the Spirit from works of the law, or from faith in what you heard?" (Gal 3:1–2).

At this point, I have a confession to make. The word of God is "a double-edged sword" (Heb 4:12). It cuts both sides—that is, it cuts the one who stands in front and the one who is holding it! Before proclaiming the word of God, says Ezekiel, it is necessary to have swallowed the scroll and filled the belly with it (Ez 3:1–3). Before experiencing it as sweet as honey on the lips, one must feel it as bitter as gall in the stomach (Rv 10:9). What a cold shower for the writer when he becomes aware, as by a sudden flash, that one of the weavers is himself and the rough cloth suit is the chapter he is writing against the weavers of their own justice!

Something similar also happened to the Apostle, precisely as he was writing his Letter to the Romans. He realized that the law of the flesh, self-complacency, was also lurking within him and exclaimed: "Unfortunate me! Who will deliver me from this body [that is, from this situation] of death? . . . With my reason I serve the law of God, but with my flesh the law of sin" (Rom 7:24–25).

Only Christ can say with absolute truth: "I do not seek my own glory" (Jn 8:50); all the others can only say: "I do not *want to seek* my own glory!" When the Apostle protests, saying, "Am I perhaps seeking the favor of men?" (Gal 1:10), what he claims is the firm decision of his "reason," not what he experiences in his "flesh." (Some resentful phrases of the same Letter to the Galatians are proof of this!) Luther's formula according to which the redeemed man is, at the same time, "righteous and sinful" (*simul justus et peccator*) is not to be rejected, if this psychological meaning is given to it and not the ontological one.

Why put these things in writing instead of simply saying them to one's own confessor? Why, for the same reason the Apostle did not hesitate to reveal his interior struggle to readers of Rome unknown to him! He thought that, in this way, he would encourage all those who would later recognize themselves in the same situation (which, by the way, is common to all the children of Adam). For his and our encouragement, the Apostle does not conclude, however, on this negative key. Rather, he proclaims the triumph of Christ's grace over this universal, atavistic enemy which is the search for one's own glory: "Who will free me from this body of death? Thanks are to God through Jesus Christ our Lord!" (Rom 7:25).

8.
Justified by Faith

By now the way is paved for addressing the crucial issue about the theological virtue of faith, which is the justification of the sinner by grace through faith in Christ.[1] We cannot help but reread the passage from the Letter to the Romans which is the text par excellence of this truth of faith:

> But now the righteousness of God has been manifested apart from law, although the law and the prophets bear witness to it, the righteousness of God through faith in Jesus Christ for all who believe. For there is no distinction; since all have sinned and fall short of the glory of God, they are justified by his grace as a gift, through the redemption which is in Christ Jesus, whom God put forward as an expiation by his blood, to be received by faith. This was to show God's righteousness, because in his divine forbearance he had passed over former sins; it was to prove at the present time that he himself is righteous and that he justifies him who has faith in Jesus. Then what becomes of our boasting? It is excluded. On what principle? On the principle of works? No, but on the principle of faith. For we hold that a man is justified by faith apart from works of law. (Rom 3:21–28)

---

1. I reproduce here the essentials of a sermon delivered to the Pontifical Household, in the presence of Pope Francis, in Lent 2017, at the occasion of the fifth centenary of the Protestant Reformation. The integral text has been published in *Journal of Ecumenical Studies* 53, no. 3 (Summer 2018): pp. 423–435, and in *Stimmen der Zeit* 142 (October 2017): pp. 669–679.

How could it happen that such a clear and comforting message became the bone of contention at the heart of Western Christianity, splitting the Church and Europe into two different religious continents? Even today, for the average believer in certain countries, that doctrine constitutes the dividing line between Catholicism and Protestantism. By those who began the Reformation, this doctrine was considered to be "the article by which the Church stands or falls" (*articulus stantis et cadentis Ecclesiae*).

We need to go back to Martin Luther's famous "tower experience" that took place in 1511 or 1512. Luther was in torment, almost to the point of desperation and resentment toward God, because all his religious and penitential observances did not succeed in making him feel accepted by God and at peace with him. It was here that, suddenly, St. Paul's word in Romans 1:17 flashed through his mind: "The just shall live by faith." Remembering this experience when he was close to death, he wrote, "When I discovered this, I felt I was reborn, and it seemed that the doors of paradise opened up for me."[2]

A question immediately arises: How do we explain the earthquake that was caused by the position Luther took? What was there about it that was so revolutionary? St. Augustine had given the same explanation for the expression "righteousness of God" many centuries earlier. "The righteousness of God [*justitia Dei*]," he wrote, "is the righteousness by which, through his grace, we become justified, exactly the way that the salvation of God [*salus Dei*] (Ps 3:9) is the salvation by which God saves us."[3] St. Gregory the Great had said, "We do not attain faith from virtue but virtue from faith."[4] St. Thomas Aquinas went even further. Commenting on the Pauline saying that "the letter kills, but the Spirit gives life" (2 Cor 3:6), he wrote that the "letter" also includes the moral

---

2. Martin Luther, "Preface to His Latin Works," Weimar ed., vol. 54, p. 186.

3. Augustine, *On the Spirit and the Letter*, 32, 56 (PL 44, 237).

4. Gregory the Great, *Homilies on Ezekiel*, 2, 7 (PL 76, 1018).

precepts of the Gospel, so "even the letter of the gospel would kill if the grace of faith that heals were not added to it."[5]

The Council of Trent, convened in response to the Reformation, did not have any difficulty in reaffirming the primacy of faith and grace while still maintaining the necessity of works and the observance of the laws in the context of the whole process of salvation, according to the Pauline formula of "faith working through love" (*"fides quae per caritatem operatur"*) (Gal 5:6).[6] This explains how, in the context of the new climate of ecumenical dialogue, it was possible for the Catholic Church and the Lutheran World Federation to arrive at a joint declaration on justification by grace through faith that was signed on October 31, 1999, which acknowledges a fundamental, if not yet total, agreement on that doctrine.

So, was the Protestant Reformation a case of "much ado about nothing"—the result of a misunderstanding? We need to answer with a firm "No!" It is true that the Magisterium of the Catholic Church had never reversed any decisions made by preceding councils (especially against the Pelagians); it had never forgotten what Augustine, Gregory, Bernard, and Thomas Aquinas had written. Human revolutions do not break out, however, because of ideas or abstract theories but because of concrete historical situations, and unfortunately for a long time, the praxis of the Church was not truly reflecting its official doctrine. Church life, catechesis, Christian piety, spiritual direction, not to mention popular preaching—all these things seemed to affirm just the opposite, that what really matters is, in fact, works, human effort. In addition, "good works" were not generally understood to mean the works listed by Jesus in Matthew 25, without which, he says, we cannot enter the kingdom of heaven. Instead, "good works" meant pilgrimages, votive candles, novenas, and donations

5. Thomas Aquinas, *Summa theologiae*, I-IIae, q. 106, a. 2.

6. Council of Trent, *Decretum de iustificatione*, 7, in Denziger and Schoenmetzer, *Enchridion Symbolorum*, ed. 34, n. 1531.

to the Church, and, as compensation for doing these things, indulgences. The phenomenon had deep roots common to all of Christianity, both Greek and Latin. After Christianity became the state religion, faith was something that was absorbed instinctively through the family, school, and society. It was not as important to emphasize the moment in which faith was born and a person's decision to become a believer as it was to emphasize the practical requirements of the faith—in other words, morals and behavior.

The true meaning of the expression "justice of God" in St. Paul had been lost; one read his words "God's righteousness has been revealed" and instinctively thought: "As expected, after God's wrath (Rom 1:18), now his justice is revealed, that is his just punishment!" Luther discovered, or rather rediscovered, that the expression "righteousness of God" does not indicate here his punishment, or worse, his vengeance against man, but indicates, on the contrary, the act by which God makes man upright. (He actually said "declares," not "makes" right, because he was thinking of an extrinsic and forensic justification.)

But let us leave all considerations aside to come to the most important question: Who is the author of such a revolutionary message proclaiming that the destiny of the whole of humanity has changed because of what a single person did a few years before? Reading the endless studies on the subject, one has the impression that everything begins with Paul and the religious situation around him. On the contrary, the doctrine of justification by faith is not Paul's invention but the central message of the Gospel of Christ. Martin Luther insisted on this. If this were not the case, then those who say that Paul, not Jesus, is the real founder of Christianity would be correct.

The core of the doctrine is already found in the Greek word *euangelion*, "gospel," "good news," that Paul certainly did not invent out of thin air. At the beginning of his ministry, Jesus went around proclaiming, "The time is fulfilled, and the kingdom of

God is at hand; repent, and believe in the gospel" (Mk 1:15). How could this proclamation be called "good news," joyful news, if it were only a threatening call to change one's life? What Christ included in the expression "kingdom of God"—that is, the salvific initiative by God's offer of salvation to all humanity—Paul called the "righteousness of God," but it refers to the same fundamental reality.

When Jesus said, "Repent, and believe the gospel," he was thus already teaching justification by faith. Before him, "to repent" always meant "to turn back," as indicated by the Hebrew word *shub*; it meant to turn back, through a renewed observance of the law, to the covenant that had been broken. "To repent," consequently, had a meaning that was mainly ascetic, moral, and penitential, and it was implemented by changing one's behavior. Repentance was seen as a condition for salvation; it meant "repent and you will be saved; repent and salvation will come to you." This was the meaning of "repent" up to this point, including on the lips of John the Baptist.

When Jesus speaks of repentance, *metanoia*, the moral meaning of the word moves into second place (at least at the beginning of his preaching) with respect to a new, previously unknown meaning. Repenting no longer means going back to the covenant and the observance of the law. Rather, it means taking a leap forward, entering into a new covenant, seizing this "kingdom" that has appeared, and entering into it by faith. "Repent and believe" does not point to two different, successive steps but to the same action: Repent, that is, believe; repent by believing! Repenting does not signify "mending one's ways" as much as "perceiving" something new and thinking in a new way.[7]

Innumerable sayings from the Gospel among the ones that most certainly go back to Jesus, confirm this interpretation. One

7. The humanist Lorenzo Valla (1405–1457), in his *Annotations on the New Testament*, had already highlighted this new meaning of the word "metanoia" in Mark's text.

is Jesus' insistence on the necessity of becoming like children to enter the realm of heaven. A characteristic of children is that they have nothing to give and can only receive. They do not ask something from their parents because they have earned it but simply because they know they are loved. They accept what is freely given. The story of the tax collector who returns home from the temple "justified" (Lk 18:14: the same term used by Paul!) is a more effective way than any reasoning to proclaim that people do not become just and pleasing to God through their works, as the Pharisee thought, but through their humble trust in God.

A difference between Jesus and Paul remains—and a great one for that matter—but it is due to Jesus, not to Paul. After having preached the Kingdom, he "died for our sins and rose again for our justification" (Rom 4:25), thus giving a new and specific content to the act of faith. The essential message, however, remains the same: salvation is not an achievement of ours but a gift from God; it is not obtained with the works of the law but with faith in Christ Jesus.

9.
The Bold Stroke of Faith

What can we conclude from our bird's-eye view of the five centuries since the beginning of the Protestant Reformation? It is vital that we do not remain prisoners of the past, trying to determine rights and wrongs, even if that is done in a more irenic tone than in the past. Instead, we need to take a leap forward if we want to respond to the new challenges Christianity is facing today. The situation has changed since then. The chief issues that provoked the separation between the Church of Rome and the Reformation were, above all, indulgences and how sinners are justified. Can we say that these are the problems on which people's faith stands or falls today?

A negative effect resulting from the centuries-old Western emphasis on liberation from sin and on justification of sinners (prior, in part, to Luther himself) is to have made the Gospel a gloomy proclamation. (Think of some "Christian" characters in Ibsen's plays and of Nietzsche's accusations!) Secular culture ended up resisting and rejecting it—and not without a reason. The most important thing, in fact, is not what Jesus, by his death, has *removed* from human beings (i.e., sin) but what he has *given* them—that is, his Holy Spirit and eternal life. "Behold the Lamb of God who takes away the sin of the world," we repeat at every Mass, with John the Baptist (Jn 1:29); but this exclamation is followed, as in a single breath, by another exclamation of the Precursor: "This is the one who baptizes in the Holy Spirit!" (Jn 1:33). Many modern exegetes rightly consider the third chapter of the Letter to the

Romans on justification by faith to be inseparable from the eighth chapter on the gift of the Holy Spirit and the new life. While instituting the Eucharist, Jesus says, it is true, that his blood is "poured out for the remission of sins"; but immediately before he has called it "the blood of the covenant" (Mt 26:28). We know the rich and glorious meaning of the "new and eternal covenant," and the place the Holy Spirit has in it (Ez 36:26–27; 2 Cor 3:6).

This doesn't mean ignoring the enrichment brought up by the Reformation or wanting to return to the situation before it. It means, rather, allowing all of Christianity to benefit from its many important achievements, once they are freed from certain distortions and excesses caused by the need to correct major abuses, as well as the overheated climate of the moment (denial of free will, total corruption of human nature because of Adam's sin). Neither is it a question of merging together, but rather of living the differences in a reconciled way.

The free gift of justification through faith in Christ should be preached today by the whole of Christianity and with more vigor than ever. This should not be done, however, in contrast to the "works" whereof the New Testament speaks but in contrast to the claim of postmodern people of being able to save themselves with their science and technology or with an improvised, comforting spirituality. These are the "works" on which many modern people rely. I am convinced that, if Luther came back to life, this would be the way that he, too, would preach justification by faith today.

The most important thing, however, is not to *preach* justification through faith but to *experience* it. There is a thing we all—Protestants and Catholics—should learn from the man who initiated the Reformation. For Luther, as we saw, the free gift of justification by faith was, first of all, a lived experience and only later something about which to theorize. After him, justification through faith increasingly became a theological thesis to defend or to oppose and less and less a personal, liberating experience to be lived out in one's intimate relationship with God. John Wesley's dramatic London experience on May 24, 1738, tells the difference between the two approaches.[1] The joint declaration of 1999 very appropriately points out that the consensus reached by Catholics and Lutherans on the fundamental truths of the doctrine of justi-fication must take effect and be confirmed not just in the teaching of the Church but also by its role in people's lives as well (no. 43).

Justification by faith is the beginning and the foundation of salvation, but a special, dynamic, not static, foundation, which must always be renewed. God is the one who justifies us every time by grace and not just once in baptism. We must therefore, again and again, accept this justification by faith. It is the law of every kind of life: we need to breathe to stay alive. We received salvation at the beginning, in Baptism, but we must continually wait for it. Paul became "righteous" when he was baptized by Ana-nias in Damascus, and so did his Galatian faithful, when they first believed. Yet he writes to them: "We expect from faith the justifi-cation we hope for" (Gal 5:5). In a homily attributed to St. John Chrysostom, we read these modern and almost existential words:

> For every man, the beginning of life is when Christ was im-molated for him. However, Christ is immolated for him at the moment he recognizes the grace and becomes conscious of the life procured for him by that immolation. [2]

Christ's death becomes actual and true for us in the moment in which we become aware of it, ratify it, rejoice in it, and give thanks for it. The liturgy suggests what we must do concretely. At Christmas time, it speaks insistently of the "admirable exchange" (*admirabile commercium*), during which God takes our humanity from us and gives us his divinity in exchange; he takes our sin from

---

1. See John and Charles Wesley, *Selected Writings and Hymns*, Paulist Press, New York, 1981, p. 107.

2. Ps.-Chrysostom, *In Pascha* (in PG 59, 723 and in SCh, 36, p. 59 s.).

us and gives us his righteousness. The most important thing is not to know the Christological doctrine of exchange. Rather, it is making such an exchange, concluding it, like someone returning home from a market, or from the stock exchange, after having made an incredible deal. The Gospel offers us a model to imitate: the tax collector we have mentioned already. He went up to the temple in a quiet hour. There were only two people around, himself and a Pharisee. He gathered his whole life into a cry and said, "O God, have mercy on me a sinner!" and "he went home justified" (Lk 18:13–14). We can do better. Put ourselves in front of a crucifix, look at it with faith, and say: "Jesus, you have taken upon yourself the sins of the world; now take mine too—past and present—and help me not to sin anymore."

Every Christian could make such an incredible deal in life! What Christ became for us—that is, "justice, sanctification and redemption" (1 Cor 1:30)—belongs to us; it is ours more than if we had done it ourselves! I am reminded of what happened toward the end of World War II, on the day the armistice of Italy was proclaimed, in September 1943. The liberation forces opened the doors of the warehouses abandoned by the retreating German army. After so many hardships and hunger, it did not seem true to the people to freely supply themselves with food and woolen blankets. I still have a vivid memory of people returning home from the city, happily carrying things on their shoulders. God invites us to do the same with the stores of his grace wide open:

> All you who are thirsty,
> come to the water!
> You who have no money,
> come, buy grain and eat;
> Come, buy grain without money,
> wine and milk without cost! (Is 55:1)

10.
Faith and Reason

Rivers of ink have been spilled around the relationship between faith and reason. The most frequent objection is that faith is incompatible with reason. As proof of this, Tertullian's saying is often quoted: "I believe because it is absurd" (*credo quia absurdum*), as if the faith of Christians were founded on the absurd and is, therefore, irrational.

Apart from the improper use that can be made of that saying, in its original context it has nothing to do with irrationalism. (The term "absurd" itself is absent in it!) It is the affirmation of the "mystery," which is above reason but not contrary to it. Nothing more than a comment—in strong colors, according to the author's style—of the Pauline saying: "I am not ashamed of the Gospel" (Rom 1:16 and 1 Cor 1:18–25). He says:

> The Son of God was crucified:
> I'm not ashamed, precisely because one should be ashamed.
> The Son of God is dead:
> it is to be believed precisely because it is incredible!
> Buried, he is resurrected:
> it is certain because it is impossible.[1]

"Incredible" and "impossible," of course, humanly speaking! The debates on faith and reason—more exactly, on reason and revelation—are affected by a radical dissymmetry. The believer

1. Tertullianus, *De carne Christi*, V, 4.

shares reason with the atheist; the atheist does not share faith in the revelation with the believer. The believer speaks the language of the atheist interlocutor; the atheist does not speak the language of the believing counterpart. Because of that, the fairest debate on faith and reason is the one that takes place in the same person, between one's faith and one's reason. We have famous cases in the history of human thought of people in whom an identical passion for both reason and faith cannot be doubted: Augustine of Hippo, Thomas Aquinas, Blaise Pascal, Søren Kierkegaard, John Henry Newman, and more recently, Simone Weil, to mention just the most famous among them. The conclusion each of them arrived at is that the supreme act of human reason is to recognize that there is something beyond it. It is also what most ennobles reason because it indicates its ability to transcend itself. Faith is not *opposed* to reason but it *supposes* reason, just as "grace supposes nature."[2]

There is a second misunderstanding to be clarified regarding the dialogue between faith and reason. The common criticism addressed to believers is that they cannot be objective, since their faith imposes on them, from the start, the conclusion to arrive at. In other words, it acts as a pre-understanding and a prejudice. Attention is not paid to the fact that the same prejudice also acts, in the opposite direction, in the nonbelieving scientist or philosopher, and perhaps in a stronger way. If you take for granted that God does not exist, the supernatural does not exist, and miracles are impossible then your conclusion is also predetermined from the start.

An exemplary case is the Resurrection of Christ. No event of antiquity is supported by as many firsthand testimonies as this, and by personalities of the intellectual caliber of Saul of Tarsus, who had previously persecuted those who did believe in it. He provides a detailed list of witnesses, some of whom were still alive

2. Thomas Aquinas, *S. Th.*, I, q. 2, a. 2 ad 1.

and could easily disprove him (1 Cor 15:6–9). Discrepancies regarding places and times of the appearances are often stressed without realizing that the unplanned coincidence is a proof (for me among the most convincing!) in favor of the historical truth of the central fact, not against it. No "pre-established harmony" in them! Appearances are not, of course, the only proof. The Apostles did not expect the sudden reversal. How, then, can we explain their sudden resolution to "go into all the world and preach the Gospel," ready to suffer and die for the name of Jesus? And how can we explain that in a short time their message changed the world? Does not denying the Resurrection of Christ force us to admit a greater miracle than the one we would avoid accepting? Nothing can be opposed to these facts except the conviction that the Resurrection of Christ is something supernatural and that the supernatural cannot exist, which is nothing but an *a priori* and a prejudice.[3]

Let us mention a lower case than the Resurrection of Christ, but one that is closer to us. Knowing the vision Freud had of reality, could he admit that the "universal love" of Francis of Assisi had a supernatural component called grace? Of course not, and in fact, he makes it a "derivation of genital love." St. Francis is just "the one who went furthest in using love for the benefit of his internal feeling of happiness."[4] In other words, he loved God, men, all creation, and, in a very special way, the crucifix because this gave him pleasure and made him feel good![5]

Modern people, instead of the truth, place the search for truth

---

3. It is sad to see how some New Testament scholars, at this point, retreat or beat around the bush ("The *cause* has risen, not the *person* of Jesus"). As if, contrary to what the Apostle writes (1 Cor 15:14), something could stand of Christianity without the Resurrection of Christ!

4. S. Freud, *Civilization and Its Discontents*, IV.

5. Freud explains all human action with the search for one's own happiness, but he does not explain the reason for this universal "drive." According also to St. Augustine, what all men have in common is the pursuit of happiness (*Conf.* X, 23, 33: "Omnes esse beati volumus"), and he gives this explanation for it: "You made us for yourself, Lord, and our heart is restless until it rests in you" (*Conf.* I, 1). Closer to him were the poet Schiller and the musician Beethoven, who praise joy as the "beautiful spark of gods," gift of "a tender Father" living "beyond the stars."

as a supreme value. Lessing has written: "If God were to grasp all truth in his right hand, and in his left, only ever-living aspiration to the truth, were it even on condition of being eternally wrong, and he were to say to me: 'Choose!', I should humbly bow toward the left saying: 'This one, Father! Pure truth belongs to you alone."[6]

The reason for this is quite simple. As long as you are researching it, it is you who leads the game as the protagonist, while in the presence of the Truth recognized as such, you no longer have a chance and must pay "the obedience of faith." Faith posits the absolute, while reason would like to indefinitely continue the discussion. Like the Scheherazade of *One Thousand and One Nights*, human reason always has a new story to tell to delay its surrender.

There are only two resolutions to the tension between faith and reason: either to reduce faith "within the limits of pure reason" or to break the limits of pure reason and "put out into the deep." A bit like when Dante's Ulysses reached the "Pillars of Hercules," once considered to be the end of the earth, and decided not to stop there but rather to make wings out of the oars for a bold flight.[7]

I must, however, be coherent with my own premises. The discourse on faith and reason, before it becomes a debate between "us and them," between believers and nonbelievers, must be a debate between believers themselves. More useful than controversy and apologetics, in this case, is self-criticism. The worst kind of rationalism, in fact, is not the external but the internal one. St. Paul wrote to the Corinthians: "My message and my proclamation were not with persuasive words of wisdom, but with a demonstration of spirit and power, so that your faith might rest not on human wisdom but on the power of God" (1 Cor

---

6. G. Lessing, *Eine Duplik*, I, in *Werke* 3, Zurich, 1974, p.149.

7. See *Inferno*, XXVI, 125: "We of the oars made wings for our mad flight" (trans. Henry Wadsworth Longfellow).

2:4–5), and again: "The weapons of our battle are not of flesh but are enormously powerful, capable of destroying fortresses. We destroy arguments and every pretension raising itself against the knowledge of God, and take every thought captive in obedience to Christ" (2 Cor 10:3–5).

What the Apostle feared has often occurred among us. Theology, especially in the West, has increasingly distanced itself from the power of the Spirit, to rely on human wisdom. Modern rationalism demanded that Christianity present its message in a dialectical way—that is, submitting it, in all respects, to research and discussion, so that it could be part of the general effort, philosophically acceptable, of a common and ever provisional self-understanding of human destiny and of the universe. But in doing so, the proclamation about the death and Resurrection of Christ is submitted to a different—and supposedly superior—instance. It is no longer a *kerygma* but only a *hypothesis*.

It is written that "the Word became flesh," but in theology, under the influence of the prevailing idealism, the Word often became just *idea*! The living God has been reduced to the *idea* of the living God (which is quite a different thing!) and the Holy Spirit to the Hegelian *idea* of the "Absolute Spirit." Pascal's distinction between "the God of Abraham, Isaac, and Jacob" and the "God of philosophers" is all about that. One no longer lives in the company of realities, but of their images, like a photographer in his darkroom, surrounded by the colorless "negatives" of his shots.

The danger inherent to this approach to theology is that God is objectified. He becomes an object we talk about, not a subject with whom—or in whose presence—we talk. A "he"—or worse, an "it"—never a "you"! It is the backlash of having made of theology a "science." The first duty of those who do science is to be neutral toward the object of their research; but can you be neutral when you are dealing with God? This was the main reason that led me, at a certain point of my life, to abandon the academic teaching of theology and to dedicate myself full time to preaching. The consequence of that way of doing theology, in fact, is that it becomes more and more a dialogue with the academic elite of the moment and less and less a nourishment for the faith of the people of God.

From that "dark chamber" we only go out with prayer, speaking *to* God before speaking *of* God. "If you are a theologian you will truly pray, and if you truly pray you are a theologian," an ancient Father used to say.[8] St. Augustine made his most enduring—and his safest!—theology while speaking *to* God in his *Confessions*. The contemplation and imitation of the Mother of God is also helpful. She never had anything to do with abstract ideas about God and her Son Jesus but only with their living reality.

8. Evagrius Ponticus, *De oratione*, 60 (PG 79, 1180).

11.
The Risk of Faith

Let us leave behind the high-profile theme of "faith and reason" to deal with another obstacle that faith must overcome, one that is more down-to-earth, if you like, but more widespread: the risk that faith is not true; put simply, that there is nothing after death! An apologetic answer to this obstacle, made famous by Blaise Pascal, is that of the "calculated risk" or the advantageous bet. In the uncertainty, he says, you should bet on the existence of God because "if you win you have won everything, if you lose, you have lost nothing."[1]

This is very true; however, it is not yet faith but, in fact, "calculation," or at most an argument in favor of the reasonableness of believing. No, the real risk of faith is another. It is the possibility (so close at hand and so fashionable today) to refuse to believe, to consider faith a naïve and prescientific explanation of reality. A matter, in any case, of secondary importance, like those people invited to the banquet of the king who apologize in turn, one saying that he had bought a field, another that he had bought five pairs of oxen, and yet another that he had just married (Lk 14:16–20).

Scripture points to yet another type of risk that is not present among poor peasants grappling with problems of oxen and fields but among people of higher education. I am alluding to what happened in Athens on the occasion of the memorable discourse of the Apostle Paul at the Areopagus (Acts 17:16–33).

1. Blaise Pascal, *Pensées*, 233, ed. Brunschvicg.

On his first journey out of Asia and toward Europe, Paul arrives in Athens. He asks and is granted an address to the intellectual aristocracy of the city gathered in the Areopagus. He starts speaking of the one God who created the universe and of whom "we too are offspring." Those present catch an allusion to the verse of one of their poets and follow him attentively. But then Paul comes to the point. He speaks of a man whom God has appointed as universal judge, proving this by raising him from the dead. The spell is over! "When they heard about the resurrection of the dead, some began to scoff, but others said, 'We should like to hear you on this some other time.'"

What disturbed them so much? First of all, the idea of the resurrection from the dead. Plato had taught them that the body (*soma*) is the tomb (*sema*) of the soul and therefore unworthy of being carried along even after death. But perhaps even more, they were baffled by the statement that the fate of the whole of humanity depended on a single historical event and on a concrete man. A century later, the Platonic philosopher Celsus will explain to Christians the reasons for the scandal of his Athenian colleagues: "Son of God, a man who lived a few years ago? One of yesterday or the day before yesterday? A man born in a Judean village to a poor spinner?"[2]

What is the risk of faith highlighted by this episode? To be scandalized by the humanity and humility of Christ. St. Augustine reveals what was the greatest obstacle for him to overcome in order to adhere to Christian faith: "Not being humble, I could not accept the humble Jesus as my God."[3] Jesus had spoken of the possibility of being "scandalized" by him because of his distance from the idea that men (including his precursor John the Baptist) had in mind of the Messiah. "And blessed is the one," he had concluded, "who takes no offense at me" (Mt 11:6).

2. In Origen, *Contra Celsum*, I, 26 and 28; VI, 10.
3. Augustine, *Confessions*, VII, 18, 24.

Modern scandal is less ostentatious than that of the Areopagites but no less present among intellectuals. The effect, worse than rejection, is silence. I have listened to many debates about God; in the majority of them, the name of Jesus Christ was never mentioned, as if he did not belong in a discussion about God.

There is yet another "risk" for faith, much more frequent in countries with an ancient Christian tradition like mine, and it is of losing it after having once believed. Here, too, a parable (not of my invention this time) will serve to illustrate the matter better than many discourses:

> A boy sets out on a journey when it is still night, to visit a distant relative. His mother gives him a little oil lamp to light him up on the forest path. The boy sets off and the light allows him to not lose his way. But as he walks, dawn comes and the sun rises. The light from the little lamp pales and is almost no longer visible, eclipsed, as it is, by the brilliance of the sun. The boy is about to throw it away, but he remembers his mother's recommendation not to part with it for any reason. He continues to hold it in his hand. As he continues walking midday comes and then dusk. When the sun goes down and the night arrives, the light of the lamp becomes visible again and it is thanks to it that the traveler reaches his destination.

At the beginning of life, in Baptism, Holy Mother Church gave you a candle, telling you to carry it lit until death. You started your journey, became a teenager, then perhaps a university student. Other lights lit up around you—science, art, success, love—that made your little candle seem almost ridiculous, and you threw it away, or you "hid it under a bushel," out of human respect. However, for each one comes the evening of life: all those lights no longer shine; they have gone down one by one. Blessed are you, my dear child, if mindful of the recommendation of the Church your mother, you had the courage of holding fast to your faith!

12.
Faith and Science

The greatest challenge faith has to face in our age does not come from philosophy, as in the past, but from science. It is breaking news these days (as I am writing): a telescope launched into space on December 25, 2021, and positioned one and a half million kilometers from the earth, relayed astonishing images of the universe on July 12, 2022, that sent the scientific world into raptures. Here are some of the reactions circulating on the Internet:

> The James Webb telescope, named so in honor of a former NASA director, has opened a new window to the cosmos, capable of catapulting us further back in time than has been possible before, until shortly after the initial Big Bang of the world. It is the most detailed view of the early universe ever obtained. It represents the first taste of a new and revolutionary astronomy that will reveal the universe as we have never seen it before.

We would be foolish and ungrateful if we did not participate in the just pride of humanity for this as for any other scientific discovery. Only the believer is able to grasp all the greatness of these human achievements because he sees in them the fulfillment of the task assigned by God to humanity to "dominate the earth" (Gn 1:28). If faith is born from amazement, these scientific discoveries should not diminish the possibility of believing but increase it. If he lived today, the Psalmist would sing with even greater enthusiasm:

> The heavens declare the glory of God;
> the firmament proclaims the works of his hands. (Ps 19:2)

God wanted to give us a tangible sign of his infinite greatness with the immensity of the universe and a sign of its "elusiveness" with the smallest particle of matter which, even once reached, physics assures us, maintains its "uncertainty." If it is no longer the beauty of creation that speaks of God to us (Wis 13:1–9), well, let it be at least his incommensurability! "Not to be limited by what is greatest and to be contained by what is smallest"[1]: this prerogative is called "divine" because it is realized ontologically only in God. In all other cases, it is just a program of life or an aesthetic ideal.[2]

When, from the stellar spaces and distances, the gaze is lowered to us human beings, one is forced to exclaim with another Psalmist:

> When I see your heavens, the work of your fingers,
> the moon and stars that you set in place—
> What is man that you are mindful of him,
> and a son of man that you care for him? (Ps 8:4–5)

"What is man?" A well-known unbelieving scientist has replied: "I always thought I was insignificant. Knowing the size of the Universe, I realize how much this is true. . . . We are just a bit of mud on a planet that belongs to the sun." A believing scientist (for Blaise Pascal was both a scientist and a believer!), on the contrary, replies:

1. "Non coerceri a maximo, contineri tamen a minimo, divinum est."
2. Ignatius of Loyola chose the motto as the epitaph on his grave and the German poet Hölderlin placed it as an inscription in his novel *Hyperion.*

Man is just a reed, the most fragile of nature; but a reed that thinks. The entire universe does not need to arm itself to annihilate it; a vapor, a drop of water [in the blood] is enough to kill him. But, even if the universe crushed him, man would still be nobler than the one who kills him, because he knows he is dying, and he knows the superiority that the universe has over him; while the universe knows nothing about it.[3]

Scientists should be the first to recognize this. They know everything (or, at least, a lot of things) about the universe and the atom; the universe and the atom know nothing about them! What would the universe be without us humans? An immense orchestra that plays a wonderful symphony that no one, not even those who play it, are able to hear! Thanks to their reason and their freedom, the ontological gap that separates human beings from God is lesser than the one that separates human beings from the rest of creation. One is almost afraid of blaspheming in formulating a similar thought, but this is the necessary consequence of the fact that, by grace, we have become "partakers of the divine nature" (2 Pt 1:4). We Christians have a reason that transcends all others: the Son of God became man! Humanity is united with God in one single person.

As usual, we make these reflections on faith and science not to convince nonbelieving scientists (none of them will ever read them) but to confirm us believers in our faith. It is the same purpose for which St. Luke tells the "illustrious Theophilus" that he wrote his Gospel: "So that you can realize the certainty of the teachings you have received" (Lk 1:4).

St. Augustine left us a kind of method in order to rise from creatures to the Creator. It consists in reviewing all creatures and picking up the cry of each of them: "Search above us. . . . I questioned, about my God, the mass of the universe, and it replied: 'I

3. Blaise Pascal, *Pensées*, 347, ed. Brunschvicg.

do not exist by myself, he made me.'"[4] It is the *quality* of being, not the *quantity*, that decides, and the quality of creation is to be . . . created! Billions of galaxies, billions of light years distant from each other, do not change this quality.

Christians are sometimes reproached for believing in the "absurd." I think that there is nothing more "absurd," if you think about it, than the idea of the "spontaneous creation" of the universe. The idea of creation from nothing is rejected while the idea of nothing creating something is found plausible! One of the most self-evident and universally shared truths is that "acting follows being" (*agere sequitur esse*). In the hypothesis of spontaneous creation, acting would precede being! And if one insists that being and acting, in the case of the universe, are simultaneous and coincide, then one has just given another name to God.

Believers are not ostriches who hide their head in the sand so as not to see. They share with each human person their bewilderment in front of the many mysteries and contradictions of the physical universe, of history, of the Bible itself, and above all the presence of evil and suffering in the world. However, they are able to overcome every perplexity with a certainty stronger than all uncertainties, which is the credibility of the person of Christ and "the power of his Resurrection" (Phil 3:10).

The story of the new, powerful telescope should arouse in us the desire for another kind of telescope that not only sees "ten times farther" than the previous ones but arrives where no human telescope can arrive. And that telescope is faith.

---

4. Augustine, *Confessions*, X, 6, 9: "Quaere super nos. . . . Non ego sum, sed ipse me fecit."

13.
Mary, Our Mother in Faith

In the *Magnificat* Mary exclaims:

> He has shown might with his arm,
> dispersed the arrogant of mind and heart.
> He has thrown down the rulers from their thrones
> but lifted up the lowly.
> The hungry he has filled with good things;
> the rich he has sent away empty. (Lk 1:51–53)

One is tempted to object: "May the honor due to you, Holy Mother of God, always be saved, but where and when did the Almighty do all the things you are saying? It was you who were sent back empty-handed when you knocked on the doors of Bethlehem, you who had to flee while the mighty Herod remained firm on his throne!"

The fact is that Mary (or rather, the Holy Spirit, who put the canticle upon her lips) invites us to rise from our human perspective to God's point of view and to see already realized that justice which is not found in history. The revolution that Mary sings about took place in history, but it is only grasped by those who look at history with the eye of faith. True, we can grasp something also "with the naked eye"—that is, by looking at what happened next. Where is the mighty Herod now? Where are the rich who found lodging in the inn of Bethlehem that night? Thrown down from their thrones, swept away, or rated as the "villains" of the tale!

Unfortunately, what had happened with the divinity of Jesus happened also with regard to Mary's faith. Since the Arian heretics sought every occasion to question the full divinity of Christ, in order to remove any pretext, the Fathers gave sometimes a "pedagogical" explanation of those texts of the Gospel that seemed to admit a progress in Jesus' knowledge of the Father's will and in his obedience to it. One of these texts was that of the Letter to the Hebrews, according to which Jesus "learned obedience from the things he suffered" (Heb 5:8) and another was the prayer of Jesus in Gethsemane. In Jesus, everything had to be given and perfect from the start. As good Greeks, they thought that *becoming* could not affect *being*.

The same, I said, happened to Mary's faith. It was taken for granted that she had made her act of faith at the moment of the Annunciation and remained in it all her life, like someone who, right at the beginning, reaches the highest note with her voice and then keeps it uninterrupted for the rest of the song. A reassuring explanation was given of all the words that seemed to say the opposite. The gift that the Holy Spirit gave to the Church, with the renewal of Mariology, was the discovery of a new dimension of Mary's faith. The Mother of God—the Second Vatican Council affirmed—"advanced in the pilgrimage of faith" (*Lumen Gentium*, 58). She did not believe once and for all, but she walked in the faith and progressed in it. The statement was taken up and made more explicit by St. John Paul II in the encyclical *Redemptoris Mater*:

> Elizabeth's words: "And blessed is she who believed" do not apply only to that particular moment of the Annunciation. Certainly this represents the culminating moment of Mary's faith in expectation of Christ, but it is also her starting point,

from which she begins her entire journey towards God, her entire journey of faith. (*RM*, 14)

On this journey, Mary reached the "night of faith" (*RM*, 18). The words of St. Augustine on Mary's faith are known and often repeated: "By faith she gave birth to what she had conceived by faith."[1] We must complete the list with what happened after the Annunciation and Christmas. By faith she presented the child to the temple; by faith she followed him in his public life, keeping a low profile; by faith she stood under the cross; and by faith she awaited his Resurrection.

Let us reflect on some moments of the journey of faith of the Mother of God. What the angel announces to her is something unheard of: it never happened before her and it will never happen after her. What is her reaction? She was "very troubled" at the words (Lk 1:29). The term used in the Gospel indicates a profound shock, as when life suddenly takes a whole new turn. The angel's response—"The Holy Spirit will descend on you"— is enough for her to pronounce her total, unconditional "yes": "Here is the servant of the Lord." She, too, sets out on her journey like Abraham, without knowing where she is going; she does not know what God has in store for her, but she accepts without hesitation.

Then comes the moment of joyful enthusiasm for Mary: a time in which everything flourishes and is amplified in joy! It is the moment of her meeting with Elizabeth. The praises she receives are very broad. Mary does not refuse them, but she sends them back to God with the *Magnificat*. It is easy to live the faith in these privileged moments, but others also come for her, moments of trial and darkness in which she is educated in a more demanding faith. There are apparently conflicting facts that Mary confronts within herself, without understanding. He is "the Son

---

1. Augustine, *Sermons*, 215: "quem credendo peperit, credendo concepit."

of God" and lies in a manger! She keeps everything in her heart and lets it ferment in expectation. She lives in the constant newness of God's plan. She hears Simeon's prophecy and soon realizes how true he was! All the ups and downs of her Son's life, all the misunderstandings and the progressive desertions around him, had profound repercussions in the heart of his mother. She first experienced this in the loss of Jesus in the temple: "'Why were you looking for me?' But they did not understand" (Lk 2:49).

Finally, there is the cross. She is there, helpless in the face of her son's martyrdom, but she agrees in love. It is a replica of Abraham's drama, but how immensely more demanding! With Abraham, God stops at the last moment; with her, he does not. She accepts that her son is to be immolated and she hands him over to the Father with a broken heart, but on her feet, strong in her unshakable faith. It is here that Mary's voice reaches its highest note. Of Mary, we must say with much greater reason what, in Romans 4:18, the Apostle says of Abraham: Mary believed, hoping against all hope, and thus she became the mother of many peoples. Our mother in faith!

It has been written that "the one who believes in Christ is obliged to become his contemporary in his lowering."[2] The meaning is that to understand what it really means to believe, one must put oneself in the shoes of those to whom Jesus addressed his words for the first time. It is relatively easy to believe when you have two thousand years of confirmation and an infinite series of signs, but what could the Apostles think when they heard the invitation "Come to me, all you who are weary and oppressed, and I will give you refreshment" (Mt 11:28) being pronounced by someone who himself did not have a stone on which to lay his head? Mary is, par excellence, the one who believed as a contemporary, when things happened for the first time, and they were things so out of the ordinary!

2. Søren Kierkegaard, *Training in Christianity*, I, E.

At the end of his sermon on Mary's faith, St. Augustine addresses an exhortation to his listeners that also applies to us: "Mary believed and in her what she believed came true. Let us too believe, so that what happened in her can also be beneficial to us."[3]

---

3. Augustine, *Sermons*, 215, 4.

14.
In Praise of Faith

What a great thing is faith! It is the hidden treasure, the precious pearl; it makes our heart a dwelling place for Christ (Eph 3:17). Jesus was always moved when he met men and women of great faith: the Canaanite, the Centurion. Faith is a gift and a necessity for salvation: "Without faith it is impossible to please God" (Heb 11:6). It is a gift that constitutes the beginning of a friendship with God; but it must be accepted, considered as something precious, nourished by one's own research and prayer, and by grace. It is a divinely complete gift because it illuminates the intelligence, moves the will, and strengthens weakness.

Faith is a seed that needs to grow; it works within you to the extent that you allow it and you set to work to welcome it, irrigating the soil. Botanists are amazed at all that is contained in a small seed. If all the information contained in a seed were to be written down, the result would be a kind of encyclopedia. Everything is planned down to the smallest detail. One thinks of a natural computer in which an incalculable amount of data is stored: when and how to blossom, which fruits to bear, of what color and flavor, what size, how to react to this or that external agent, how to adapt to a different climate. Sometimes all this information remains operative for centuries and millennia, if the news is true that wheat seeds still alive and capable of germinating were found in the ancient pyramids of Egypt.

Well, the revealed message is also a seed. Jesus himself compares it to "the least of all seeds" (Mt 13:32) and compares himself to a grain of wheat sown on the ground (Jn 12:24). Like the seed, it hides within itself unsuspected resources that after two thousand years we are far from having finished exploring. Like the natural seed, it too knows how to adapt to any terrain and any climate! No one will ever be able to delude himself by thinking that he has said everything about it and that there is nothing more to say or to discover.

Faith is a continuous stimulus toward holiness; it is a calm impatience that does not allow you to rest on your laurels. It is a light that reveals the disorder and dirt that lurk in your soul; it is a sun that burns to ripen. Of course, those who had looked for it as an anesthetic will be disappointed. They get scared and sometimes pull back.

Faith transforms, purifies, and improves. If this does not happen, it is the sign that it is a weak faith. We know Abraham's transformation from shepherd to father in faith; of Levi, from publican to Apostle; of Zacchaeus, from stingy usurer to a generous donor of his possessions; of Mary Magdalene, from a love that leaves you restless to the love that satisfies; of the Samaritan woman, from a woman of easy virtue to the witness of the Messiah; of Paul, from persecutor to an apostle to the Gentiles; of Augustine and an interminable crowd of men and women who have welcomed faith as a precious pearl and have valued it with the necessary dispositions of mind.

Faith makes you discover a new way of loving, a new way of living, working, serving, praying, speaking, suffering, and rejoicing—a new way of being! It makes you a new man and a new woman. It accompanies you to the threshold of eternity and then vanishes, disappears, but not before having given you what you believed in, the eternal possession of God and endless happiness.

Faith is the hand that the king of the universe extends to the poor, and the poor extend to their benefactor. Between the Creator and the creature there is "an infinite qualitative distance," but when God stretches out his hand, the distance is canceled. As it happens at the conclusion of every covenant, salvation consists in a handshake.

In the electronic age, we have a new image of faith: the internet connection. As soon as I arrived at a certain destination in my preaching journeys in Italy and abroad, my first concern was to look for an internet connection to receive emails, find news and information, and be in contact with my community. This often presented difficulties, due to my lack of know-how in the matter; I had to make several attempts and ask for help before succeeding. When the Google sign-in page finally appeared on the screen, I breathed a sigh of relief. I was connected and the whole virtual world opened up in front of me. Something similar is achieved by faith. Wirelessly, effortlessly, expense-free. A short prayer, a simple movement of the heart, and we are connected to a world that is not just virtual but real, the world of God! Connected not through the ether but through the Holy Spirit.

Believing is a possibility offered to everyone, without distinction. It is the only thing that realizes equality among people because everyone—rich and poor, learned and ignorant—has the same ability to believe. Indeed, the poor, the simple, and the disadvantaged, from the human point of view, are often the most privileged in relation to faith. Jesus said words that, alone, explain the incredulity of so many scholars, today and in the past:

> I give praise to you, Father, Lord of heaven and earth,
> for you have hidden these things from the wise and the learned
> and you have revealed them to the childlike. (Mt 11:25)

Part Two

THOSE WHO HOPE IN THE LORD

The Gate of Hope

15.
The Beautiful Gate

The temple of Jerusalem had a gate called "the Beautiful Gate" (Acts 3:2). Also, the temple of God that is our heart has a beautiful gate: it is the door of hope that we want now to open to Christ who comes. "Christ in you, hope of glory" (Col 1:27): this is for Paul a kind of summary of the whole Christian life.

Strangely enough, the word "hope" is absent from Jesus' preaching. The Gospels relate many of his sayings on faith and charity but none on hope, even if—as we will see later—all his preaching proclaims that there is a resurrection from the dead and an eternal life. On the contrary, after Easter, we see the idea and the sentiment of hope literally explode in the preaching of the Apostles. Hope takes its place, alongside faith and charity, as one of the three constitutive qualities of Christian existence.

The explanation for the absence of sayings on hope in the Gospel is simple: Christ had first to die and rise again. Rising, he unsealed the source of hope; he inaugurated the very object of theological hope, which is a life with God beyond death. The Apostle Peter can say of God the Father:

> Blessed be the God and Father of our Lord Jesus Christ, who in his great mercy gave us a new birth to a living hope through the resurrection of Jesus Christ from the dead, to an inheritance that is imperishable, undefiled, and unfading, kept in heaven for you. (1 Pt 1:3–4)

67

The virtue of hope has two aspects that are inseparable but distinct from each other. To understand what they are, we need to recall the distinction I highlighted in regard to faith between *believed* faith and *believing* faith. This distinction applies also to hope. There is an objective hope that indicates the thing hoped for, and there is a subjective hope that indicates, instead, the act of hoping for something, an expectant hope. The latter is a force of forward propulsion, an inner impulse, an extension of the soul toward the future. It is "a joyful migration of the spirit towards what one hopes for," said an ancient Father of the desert.[1] This hoping with the whole being is not a *waiting* but a *seeking*. Whoever waits, stands still; he who seeks, walks and explores. Hope becomes the engine or the propeller of the spiritual life.

The two aspects of hope are clearly highlighted in the *Catechism of the Catholic Church*. In the first paragraph (§1817), dedicated to the objective aspect of virtue, we read: "Hope is the theological virtue by which we desire the kingdom of heaven and eternal life as our happiness, placing our trust in Christ's promises and relying not on our own strength, but on the help of the grace of the Holy Spirit."

In the next paragraph (§1818), dedicated to the subjective dimension of hope, we read: "The virtue of hope responds to the aspiration to happiness which God has placed in the heart of every man; it takes up the hopes that inspire men's activities and purifies them so as to order them to the Kingdom of heaven; it keeps man from discouragement; it sustains him during times of abandonment; it opens up his heart in expectation of eternal beatitude. Buoyed up by hope, he is preserved from selfishness and led to the happiness that flows from charity."

Scripture itself highlights this double meaning of the word hope. "Let us keep without wavering the profession of our hope, because he who promised is faithful" (Heb 10:23; 6:19); "There

1. Diadochus of Photike, *Capita gnostica*, preamb. (SCh 5 bis, p. 84).

is only one hope to which you have been called" (Eph 4:4). In these texts the object of hope is spoken of. "We who have hoped in Christ" (Eph 1:12): here we are not speaking of hoping for something but of hoping in someone: the subjective dimension of hope is highlighted. More than an object of having, hope appears here as a quality of being.

This is the hope spoken of in Psalm 130, the famous *De profundis*, which is the psalm of hope par excellence:

> Out of the depths I call to you, Lord . . .
> I wait for the Lord,
> my soul waits
> and I hope for his word.
> My soul looks for the Lord
> more than sentinels for daybreak.

We must redeem this psalm from the prejudice created by the tradition, at least in the Catholic Church, of reciting it regularly on the occasion of funerals and prayers for the dead. The "depths" from which the Psalmist cries out to God are not those of purgatory (this belief did not yet exist when the Psalm was composed!) but the depths of one's own misery and sin.

The cry that the Psalmist raises to God is a cry of hope that rises from someone in a moment of truth about himself or herself. It is a cry of the living, not of the dead! Personal hope ("my soul") and collective hope ("Israel") are reborn each time a person or a community acknowledges and repents of sin. Let us remember this, next time we recite this moving Psalm!

16.
Waiting for the
Blessed Hope

Let us start with the objective dimension of hope, from the Augustinian "quid sperandum," what to hope for. What is the proper object of the "blessed hope," which we proclaim to be "awaiting" at every Mass?

To realize the absolute novelty brought about by Christ in this field, we need to place the Gospel revelation against the background of ancient beliefs about the hereafter. The heretic Marcion, in the second century, addressed this provocative question to the Church: "What novelty did then the Lord come to bring us?" St. Irenaeus replies: "He brought every newness by bringing himself."[1] The person of Jesus is himself the novelty. Within this universal newness, however, there is one that touches each of us in a personal and existential way: Jesus revealed the ultimate destiny of humanity; he broke through the wall of death in the face of which all human hopes ended.

On this point, even the Hebrew Testament had no answer to give. It is well known that only toward the end of it does one have some explicit statements about a life after death. Before then, the belief of Israel did not differ from that of neighboring peoples, especially those of Mesopotamia. Death ends life forever; we all, good and bad, end up in a kind of dismal "common grave" that elsewhere is called *Arallu* and in the Bible the *Sheol*: "None of the

---

1. Irenaeus of Lyon, *Adversus Haereses*, IV, 34, 1.

dead remembers you. Who in *Sheol* sings your praises?" (Ps 6:6). The dominant belief in the Greco-Roman world contemporary with the New Testament is no different. It calls that sad place of shadows *Hell*, or *Hades*.

The great thing that distinguishes Israel from all other peoples is that it has continued, despite everything, to believe in the goodness and love of its God. It has not attributed death to the envy of the divinity who keeps immortality for itself (as was the case with the Babylonians), but rather to human sin (Gn 3). At certain moments, the sacred authors do not conceal their bewilderment in the face of a fate that does not seem to make any distinction between righteous and sinners. After that of Job, the most acute cry, in this sense, is that of Qoheleth (Eccl 3:19–20). However, Israel has never come to rebellion. In the end, Job too changes his mind and puts his hand over his mouth. Some Psalmists have gone so far as to desire and glimpse the possibility of a relationship with God beyond death: a being "torn from *Sheol*" (Ps 49:16), a "being with God always" (Ps 73:23–24) and "satiated with joy in his presence" (Ps 16:11).

Karl Marx spread the thesis—for atheists now almost "canonical"—according to which faith in God and in an afterlife is nothing but the projection of the unfulfilled desires of the present life. The Bible, as we can see, totally contradicts this theory. The people of Israel believed in their God many centuries before they believed in the existence of an afterlife. Hope was born from faith, not faith from hope!

When, toward the end of the Hebrew Testament, the expectation that developed in the underground of the biblical soul eventually came to light; it was not expressed as the survival of the immortal soul, which, freed from the body, returns to its original celestial world. In accord with the biblical idea of man as an inseparable unity of soul and body, survival consists in the resurrection—body and soul—from death (Dn 12:2–3; 2 Mc 7:9).

Jesus suddenly brought this faith to its fullness. In his preaching, he vigorously affirms the resurrection of the dead. In response to the Sadducees who had challenged him with the example of the woman who had had seven husbands (Lk 20:27–38), Jesus appeals to the episode of the burning bush where God proclaims himself "God of Abraham, God of Isaac, and God of Jacob," though all the three had died long before Moses. Then he concludes: "He is not God of the dead, but of the living, for to him all are alive." The strength of this argument can be put into a kind of syllogism:

> God is the God of Abraham, Isaac, and Jacob.
> But God is not the God of the dead but of the living.
> Therefore Abraham, Isaac, and Jacob are alive!

The decisive proof of the resurrection from the dead is provided, however, only by Christ's Resurrection: "If Christ is preached as raised from the dead, how can some among you say there is no resurrection of the dead?" (1 Cor 15:12).

The most precious legacy that Queen Elizabeth II of the United Kingdom left to her nation and the world, after her seventy-year reign, was her Christian hope of the resurrection from death. In her funeral rite, followed live by almost all the powerful of the earth and, on television, by hundreds of millions of people, by her express will, the words of Paul were proclaimed in the first reading:

> "Death is swallowed up in victory.
> Where, O death, is your victory?
> Where, O death, is your sting?"
> The sting of death is sin, and the power of sin is the law.
> But thanks be to God who gives us the victory
> through our Lord Jesus Christ. (1 Cor 15:54–57)

72

And, in the Gospel, again by her will, the words of Jesus:

> In my Father's house there are many dwelling places. . . . And
> if I go and prepare a place for you, I will come back again
> and take you to myself, so that where I am you also may be.
> (Jn 14:2–3)

After Christ—and thanks to him—death is no longer a landing
but a takeoff!

17.
We Shall See God
Face to Face

Precisely because we are still immersed in time and space, we lack the necessary categories to fathom what "eternal life" with God consists of. It is like wanting to explain what light is to someone who was born blind. St. Paul simply says:

> It is sown dishonorable; it is raised glorious.
> It is sown weak; it is raised powerful.
> It is sown a natural body; it is raised a spiritual body.
> (1 Cor 15:43–44)

While still on earth, some saints have been given to experience a few drops of the infinite ocean of happiness that God keeps prepared for his own; but all of them unanimously affirm that nothing can be said about it in human words. The first of them is the very Apostle Paul. He confides to the Corinthians that he was elevated fourteen years earlier (he does not know whether with his body or without it) to the "third heaven," in paradise, and that he had heard "unspeakable words that it is not lawful for anyone to pronounce" (2 Cor 12:2–4). The remembrance that such experience left in him is perceptible in what he writes on another occasion:

What eye has not seen, and ear has not heard,
and what has not entered the human heart,
God has prepared for those who love him. (1 Cor 2:9)

St. Augustine, returning from an experience similar to that
of the Apostle, writes that he retains of it "only a loving memory
and nostalgia, like the scent of a dish that one cannot yet taste."[1]
Dante compares the one who returns from such an experience
to a person who had a beautiful dream: when he wakes up, he
is unable to remember its content, but the sweetness that distills
from it remains in his heart.[2]

A famous mystic wrote that in heaven, the blessed enjoy a
special joy, the "joy of incomprehension; they understand that
they cannot understand."[3] In fact, God can be possessed but not
fully comprehended. A God understood, in fact, would no longer
be the *only* God, because to fully understand is to be equal!

But is it not written that in heaven we will see God "face-to-
face"? That we will know him perfectly, as he knows us (1 Cor
13:12), and that we will see him "as he is" (1 Jn 3:2)? All true! In
fact, he will know us for what we are: limited creatures, tiny par-
ticles of the whole, made great only by his love for us; and we will
know God for what he is: the Infinite, the Incomprehensible, and
the Ineffable. We will know him as the unknowable. "We shall
be like him" (1 Jn 3:2): similar (*homoioi*), not equal, for uniquely
the only begotten Son is perfectly equal—in the Creed we say
consubstantial (*homoousios*)—with the Father.

In the theological reflection of the Church, two tendencies
are represented. One, prevalent in Orthodox spirituality and, in
the West, in Thomistic theology, gives priority to the *vision* of

1. Augustine, *Confessions*, VII, 17, 23.
2. *Paradise*, XXXIII, 58–63.
3. Angela of Foligno (1248–1309), *Complete Works*, Paulist Press, New York, 1993, p. 239
("gaudium incomprehensibilitatis"); the same idea is found in J. Ruusbroec (1293–1381), *The
Spiritual Espousals*, II, 42.

God. The other, prevalent in Augustinian and Franciscan spirituality, puts *union* with and *enjoyment* of God first. One starts from the definition of God as light, the other from the definition of God as love. No need to choose between the two, because both are biblical and inseparable. If it is permissible, however, to express a preference, I would choose the second way. And not for the mere fact that I am a Franciscan! You cannot love without knowing, but you can know without loving! Knowledge does not necessarily include love, while love always includes knowledge: "By loving we know," "love is itself knowledge," wrote St. Gregory the Great, as a good disciple of St. Augustine.[4]

But let us leave aside what will be in the hereafter (about which we can say so little) and come instead to the present life—that is, to the exercise of the theological virtue of hope, which is what is most important for us. It is time that the passage from the Old to the New Testament, *historically* realized two thousand years ago, take place *existentially* today in each one of us, showing that the revelation of eternal life changes the life of a believer also here below.

An atheist recounted an experience of his. Out of duty to his office, he was attending a Christian funeral. At a certain point, the celebrant said in a solemn tone: "This brother will rise again; one day we all shall be raised to life!" He looked around: none of those attending had blinked an eye or showed any sign of emotion. He said to himself, "If I could believe what these people say they believe, I think I'd jump for joy and shout *Hooray! Hooray!*"

I am not saying that we can always jump for joy (we are in faith, not in vision!), but people should be able to see that faith in eternal life changes something in the life of those who believe in it, in their words and in their very gaze. The Apostle Peter suggests two things with which to radiate hope: sweetness and respect (1

---

4. Gregory the Great, *Moralia in Job*, 10, 13: "per amorem cognoscimus," and *Hom. in Evangelia* 27, 4: "amor ipse notitia est"; see Augustine, *Confessions*, VII, 10.

Pt 3:15–16). Those for whom eternal life is something more than an abstract belief, in front of every difficulty and contradiction, repeat to themselves, with St. Bernard and St. Ignatius of Loyola: "Quid hoc ad aeternitatem?" (What is this compared to eternity?)

18.
Hope, a Poor Relation Among the Theological Virtues?

Of the two components of the theological virtues, the objective and the subjective, ancient and Scholastic thought—as we once said speaking of faith—has privileged the first. It dealt with what they are in themselves, their object and their mutual relations; modern thought, instead, favors the second component, which highlights the existential dimension of the theological virtues, how they operate in those who receive them and how they relate to modern culture.

There is a simple and suggestive way to grasp the difference between the two perspectives and the enrichment that the second brings to the first. It consists in seeing how two great Christian poets have treated the theme of the theological virtues: Dante Alighieri and Charles Péguy (the juxtaposition between the two, at least on this point, should not seem arbitrary and exaggerated).

Before being admitted to the supreme vision of God, Dante must pass an examination on the three theological virtues. To question him on faith is St. Peter, on hope is St. James, and on charity is St. John. To the question of St. Peter—"Faith, what is it?"—the poet replies by putting in verse the definition of the Letter to the Hebrews (11:1):

> Faith is the substance of the things we hope for,
> And evidence of those that are not seen.[1]

That is, faith is the foundation of the things hoped for, the guarantee of those that are not yet seen. This is the definition St. Thomas Aquinas also shared.[2] The examination continues: "From what sources do we draw this faith?" And the answer is: from the pages of the Old and New Testaments, which are inspired by God.

Having passed the test on faith, the poet, in the following canto (XXV), is subjected by St. James to the examination on hope:

> Hope . . .
> Say what it is, and how it is flowering within
> Thy mind, and say from whence it came to thee.

That is: What is hope? Is your soul adorned with it and whence does it come to you? The answer—again in tune with the purest Scholastic theology—is:

> Hope, said I, is the certain expectation
> Of future glory, which is the effect
> Of grace divine and merit precedent.

Hope, like faith, is based on the divine Scriptures.

Thus, in the following canto, XXVI, we arrive at the examination on charity. The examiner could be no other but the Apostle of love, John. This time, the format is a little different and less schematic and can be put in prose.

—Tell me what is the ultimate goal to which your soul tends?

---

1. *Paradise*, XXIV, 64–65 (trans. Longfellow).
2. *S. Th.*, II-IIae, q. 4, a. 1.

—My soul tends to that good which is the beginning and end of all good.

—Who taught you to direct the arc of your desire to this goal?

—Reason and faith together, because the greater a good is, the more must it be loved; but God is the greatest good: therefore, love for him must be the greatest. So Aristotle teaches me, so does God giving Moses the first commandment, so do you too, John, in your Gospel.

—So you must reserve your supreme love for God! But tell me: are there other reasons that push you to this?

—Yes, the finiteness of the world, my own finiteness, the death on the cross that Christ endured for me: all this has helped draw me out of the sea of fallacious love and made me land on the shore of true love.

Péguy's discourse on the theological virtues also starts with an examination. The questioning, however, does not take place in heaven but on earth; the examiner is not an apostle but a poor country priest; the one being examined is a child, perhaps in preparation for the sacrament of Confirmation.

—God's minister, the priest, says: What are the three theological virtues?

—The child replies: The three theological virtues are faith, hope and charity.

—Why are faith, hope and charity called theological virtues?

—Faith, hope and charity are called theological virtues because they immediately refer to God.

—What is hope?

—Hope is a supernatural virtue for which we expect from God, with confidence, his grace in this world and eternal glory in the next.[3]

3. *Le Porche de la deuxième vertu*, Paris, Gallimard, 1975, pp. 536–537.

So far, the catechism has not changed very much since Dante's time. But here comes the man Péguy (so modern in his anti-modernism!) with his doubts, questions, perplexities, paradoxes, and distinctions. The end of the beautiful harmony between faith and reason, between the Gospel and Aristotle! The poet's stroke of genius lies in putting his questions and his preferences in the mouth of God himself.

"My favorite faith, says God, is hope."[4] Faith does not surprise me (I am paraphrasing the words of the author). I shine so much in my creation—in the sun, in the moon, and in the stars, in the lights of the firmament and in the fish of the sea—that, in order not to believe, it would require for this poor people (he is talking about us) to be blind. To believe there is only to let go, there is only to look. In order not to believe one needs to be violent, tortured, tormented, and angry. To stiffen. To take oneself upside down.

"Neither does charity amaze me that much."[5] These poor creatures (again, I am paraphrasing) are so unhappy that, unless they have a heart of stone, how could they not have a little charity for each other?

"What amazes me, says God, is hope. . . . That these poor children of mine see how things are going and believe that tomorrow it will be better, that a hundred contradictions of the facts do not distract them from still hoping, well, this really amazes me and it means that my grace must be incredibly strong."[6] (Samuel Beckett's play *Waiting for Godot* could be interpreted in this light!)

Faith, hope, and charity are three sisters who go down the street holding hands: the two bigger ones on each side and the little girl in the center. And you can guess who the girl is. Everyone, seeing them, thinks that it is the two bigger ones who are pulling

4. Ibid., p. 531.
5. Ibid., p. 534.
6. Ibid., pp. 535, 534.

the little one in the center. They are wrong! It is she, the little one, who drags everything. If hope stands still everything stands still.[7]

Little doubt remains about which of the three theological virtues the poet loves most. The real great temptation for him is that against hope; on this point, he is in agreement with classical theology, which considers despair "the gravest sin of all."[8] A doubt arises in us instead! Is it true that it is so easy to believe in God and that it is so spontaneous to love one another? The poet does not intend, I think, to talk about how things are going, but how they should go.

In any case, one merit must be given to the poet Péguy and, in general, to the modern approach to the theological virtues: that of having removed hope from the category of the "poor relation" among the theological virtues. Of the thirty-two chapters that St. Augustine dedicates to the theological virtues in his manual, the *Enchiridion*, only one, the penultimate, is dedicated to hope! St. Thomas Aquinas is a little more generous: of the forty-five questions on the theological virtues, six are dedicated to the second virtue.[9] This minor space accorded to hope in theology has an explanation. It has always been difficult to recognize hope as a virtue of its own, since its object, eternal life, seems to be nothing more than a subspecies of faith, one of its contents, precisely the one named last in the apostolic symbol: "I believe in . . . the resurrection of the body and eternal life."

The specificity of hope is best grasped if we also consider the more subjective and existential aspect of it, as highlighted by modern thought. Indeed, it is one thing to believe that there is eternal life and another to desire and experience a foretaste of that same eternal life, just as believing that God exists is different from longing for and "thirsting for God." According to our friend

7. Cf. ibid., pp. 539–540.
8. Thomas Aquinas, *S. Th.*, II-IIae, q. 20, a. 3.
9. *S. Th.*, II-IIae, qq. 17–22.

Péguy, "Faith sees only what is; hope sees what will be. Charity loves only what is, hope loves what it will be."[10]

10. Péguy, op. cit., pp. 539 and 540.

19.
God, Too, Knows Hope!

At first sight, it would seem that there is a difference and dissymmetry between the three theological virtues, much deeper than that between the ancient and the modern vision. Charity is reciprocal because God loves us and we love him. Not so, apparently, with faith and hope. We have faith and hope in God, but can God have faith and hope in us?

The answer is yes, God also has faith and hope in us! God has more faith—that is, trust—in us than we have in him (he has entrusted us with the care of all of his creation!). He has more hope in us than we have in him. God's faith and hope, like ours, will cease with our death, while love—in him and in us—remains forever (1 Cor 13:13).

Let us question the Scriptures. Jesus says: "There will be more joy in heaven over one sinner who repents than over ninety-nine righteous people who have no need of repentance" (Lk 15:7). This is a bit too strong. It is okay that there is joy and celebration in heaven for a found sheep—that is, for a sinner who is converted—but why "more joy" than for the ninety-nine left in the fold? Why does a sheep have to count on the scales as much as all the rest put together, and the one who ran away and created more problems matters most?

The explanation I find most convincing is this. By getting lost, that sheep, as well as the prodigal son, made God's heart tremble. God feared losing them forever, of being forced to condemn and deprive himself forever of them. This fear made hope in God blossom, and hope, once fulfilled, provoked joy and celebration. "Every human conversion is the crowning of a hope of God."[1]

I remember an event that took place some time ago. A three-year-old girl disappeared, and for a couple of days, nothing was heard. The most disturbing hypotheses had been made. The parents were desperate. Then, she suddenly reappeared. The television that closely followed the event managed to capture the very moment when her mother ran to meet her and hugged her to her breast, covering her with kisses. It was the very image of happiness.

This is what Jesus wanted to tell us when he speaks of God's joy for a found son! No doubt that, if they could have chosen, that mom and dad would have preferred that their little girl had never been lost (and God would have wanted the same with sinners). Once that happened, however, the return brought them a joy they would never have known if nothing had happened. In them, too, anguish had given birth to hope, and hope, when fulfilled, had caused joy to explode.

In the case of the lost sheep, the lost coin, and the departed son, God's hope was fulfilled. There are, however, disappointed hopes for God too. When Jesus said to the rich young man, "If you want to be perfect, go, sell everything you have and give it to the poor, then come and follow me," the young man went away sad (Mt 19:21). A hope remained unfulfilled. Two persons were "sad" that day! So it is for everyone, sinners and saints: we can all, at any moment, realize or frustrate a hope of God.

It may seem strange that even God knows hope. It is a mystery, but that is the way it is. In us human creatures, the condition that makes hope possible is the fact that we do not see the future. We do not know what it has in store for us, and therefore there is room in us for hope. In God, who knows the future, the condition that makes possible some form (mysterious but true)

1. Charles Péguy, *Le Porche*, cit., pp. 606–610.

of hope is that he does not want to—and, in a certain sense, cannot—achieve what he wants without our consent. Human freedom explains the existence of hope in God.

These considerations of ours are nothing more than poor attempts to approach the mystery of a God whose thoughts are not our thoughts (Is 55:8). Our thoughts on God are like midges that stubbornly rush at night against a source of light enclosed in a glass sphere and end up burning their wings and falling exhausted to the ground. But at least the thoughts we have expressed are more in conformity with what the Bible and human reason allow us to think of God. More in conformity, in any case, than the idea of a God who, in advance and from eternity, decides ("predestines"!) who he will welcome one day into his kingdom and who he will exclude from it forever. The recurrent doctrine of the "double predestination," to glory or to damnation—no matter how famous and well-meaning some of its supporters have been—is incompatible with the revelation of God as love and with his expressed will that "everyone be saved" (1 Tm 2:4). It destroys, with one stroke, both God's goodness and human freedom, objectively leading to one or the other of the two capital sins against hope. If one believes oneself, indeed, to be predestined to glory, it is *presumption,* and if one fears oneself to be predestined to damnation, it's *despair.* The only real and justified reason for despair in life![2]

Our God is a God who does not want sinners to die, but rather wants them to be converted and live (Ez 33:11). He does not want the death of the body, but even more, he does not want the eternal death of the soul. If this "second death" (Rv 2:11) will occur (I "hope" not), one thing is certain: it is not God who wanted it and decided it from the start. How reassuring are the words once addressed by Jesus to the English medieval mystic

2. At the time of Jansenism, this doctrine was the cause of a spiritual crisis for many persons, including, at a certain moment, St. Francis de Sales.

Julian of Norwich: "Sin is inevitable, but all shall be well, and all manner of things shall be well."[3]

Do we thus trivialize sin or downplay God's justice and judgment? Certainly not! We should, however, interpret spiritually the physical images of "external darkness," "gnashing of teeth," and "unquenchable fire"—that is, taking them to mean a kind of suffering immensely more serious than can be expressed with human words. This, I think, is the truth the Gospel intends to convey to us with those images comprehensible by us. We need to take into account, in addition, that the meaning of the words "eternal" and "eternity" (*aiôn*) is different in the Bible—New Testament included—from the philosophical one, familiar to us today. "Eternal" in the Bible refers to the *quality* of a life (life "in Christ," "divine life") more than its *duration*!

Hell, in conclusion, exists, and it is more terrible than we can fathom here on earth, but it isn't what people are accustomed to think. It's not the hell of Dante's *Divine Comedy*. (Nor is purgatory what we see in our devotional images of it.[4]) We are not, however, authorized to think that any human person, not even Judas, is in it. The Church declares some people "saints," none "damned." We need "despair" of no one. The final status of humanity at the very end of time is a secret God has reserved to himself. We should renounce dangerously speculating on it and rely, instead, on the rock-solid assurance that "God is love"!

Sometimes a "pure love of God" has been spoken of—that is, a love so disinterested as to be pursued regardless of one's own eternal destiny. By a special grace of God, they say, it is possible for a soul to come to a love so ardent as to love God (generally the person of Christ) only for his joy, even if he would decide to deprive him or her of his vision forever. It is not up to us to judge what happens in such souls. We know that love can cause

3. Julian of Norwich, *Revelations of Divine Love*, chap. 27.

4. St. Catherine of Genoa, with her famous treatise *On Purgatory*, puts us on the right path to see the difference between our representation and the reality.

a person to be "unreasonable." The reality, however, is that one theological virtue cannot be exercised without the other, charity without hope. "To love God selflessly," writes St. Augustine, "means to hope God from God."[5]

The important thing is to be able to say with the great Armenian mystic Gregory of Narek: "My soul is not yearning for the wedding banquet, but for the desire of the Bridegroom."[6] For love, not for interest.

5. Augustine, *Sermons*, 334, 3: "Hoc est Deum gratis amare, de Deo Deum sperare."
6. Gregory of Narek, *Book of Prayers*, nr. 12 (SCh, 78).

20.
On the Wings of Hope

Regarding the subjective component of hope, that of the "expectant hope," the most beautiful text in the New Testament is that of Paul in the Letter to the Romans, a kind of condensed *parenesis*, or exhortation, on the second theological virtue:

> May the God of hope
> fill you with all joy and peace in believing,
> so that you may abound in hope
> by the power of the holy Spirit. (Rom 15:13)

The expression "God of hope" does not only mean the God who promised eternal life and helps to achieve it or the God we hope to possess one day. It also means this, but not only this. The God of hope is also the God who allows us to hope, who opens the heart to hope; the God who fueled the relentless expectation of the prophets; the God of promise who opens up the future and pushes his people forward, to "those days"; the God who frees us from the terrible prison of time, as he liberated his people from the slavery of Pharaoh.

In the expression "God of hope," God is, at the same time, subject and object. He is the God who gives hope and who is given by hope, who is at the beginning and at the end of it. The expression has overtones that can be understood better than put in words. The same must be said of the phrase "Christ in you, the hope of glory" (Col 1:27). The risen Christ appears here as the one who gives us the strength to hope, who keeps hope alive, who is himself, with his Spirit, a fountain of living and gushing hope in the depths of our hearts. Therefore, when the Apostle says that Christians must "rejoice in hope" (Rom 12:12), it does not only mean that Christians *hope to be happy* (after death), but that they *are happy to hope*, happy already now.

This is the only way to be truly happy in this life. We can get an idea of what "rejoicing in hope" means, starting from human experience. The poet Giacomo Leopardi expressed it, as only poetry can do, in the poem "Saturday in the Village." The real joy—he says—is that of waiting, that of Saturday, when the feast is still entirely ahead; not that of Sunday when thought returns to the "usual work." At least—we must specify as believers—until the great, eternal Sunday comes for us, that "eighth day" that knows no sunset.

For two thousand years, Christians have been repeating the words of the pious Israelite who went on a pilgrimage to the holy city: "I rejoiced when they said to me, 'Let us go to the house of the Lord!'" (Ps 122:1). Christians, however, keep repeating these words thinking of another Jerusalem. St. Augustine said: "With hope, God feeds us, nourishes us, strengthens us and comforts us amidst the hardships of the present life. For this hope we sing the Alleluia. And if hope brings us such great joy, what will possessed reality be? Do you ask what will it be? Listen: 'They will be intoxicated by the abundance of your house' (Ps 36:9). This is what our hope has as its object."[1]

This hope, understood as an act, or as a state of mind and as the ability to project forward, is a mystery and a miracle, as a life that blossoms always is. It transforms everything it touches. Its effect is beautifully described in the text from Isaiah:

1. Augustine, *Sermons*, 255, 5.

Though young men faint and grow weary,
and youths stagger and fall,
They that hope in the Lord will renew their strength,
they will soar on eagles' wings;
They will run and not grow weary,
walk and not grow faint. (Is 40:30–31)

The oracle is the response to the lament of the people who say: "My fate is hidden from the Lord." God does not promise to remove the reasons for weariness and exhaustion, but he gives hope. The situation remains in itself what it was, but hope gives the strength to rise above it. It is really like putting on wings.

In the book of Revelation, we read that "when the dragon saw that it had been thrown down to the earth, it pursued the woman who had given birth to the male child. But the woman was given the two wings of the great eagle, so that she could fly to her place in the desert" (Rv 12:13–14). If the image of the eagle's wings is inspired, as it clearly seems, by the text of Isaiah, this means that the whole Church has been given the great wings of hope so that with them it can, every time, escape the attacks of evil and overcome every difficulty.

21.
Give Them a Chance!

With regard to hope, as with faith, ancient thought—both patristic and medieval—was more interested, as was said above, in the
objective aspect—that is, with the thing hoped for, eternal life;
modern thought has given preference to the subjective aspect,
asking itself what it means to hope, what the act of hoping psy-
chologically implies and how it affects our human life. I would
like to mention one of these philosophical essays on hope, that
of Kierkegaard (he, too, so modern in his anti-modernism!). Due
to the influence the author has exercised on modern thought, his
analysis can help us bring our preaching of hope closer to the people of today, more responsive to their expectations: in a certain
sense, to "inculturate" hope.

Kierkegaard starts from the assumption that there is no hope,
in the strict sense, if one does not have eternity as a horizon. Only
eternity removes all the obstacles that stand in the way of hope,
up to the last one, which is death; it assures hope that unlimited
space, which it needs and without which it cannot breathe. Millions of years are not enough. Otherwise, it turns into the anguish
of knowing that every hour that passes is something taken away
from hope. Waiting turns into a painful countdown. Now, with
the Incarnation of Christ, it has happened that eternity has entered time. Thus the very possibility of hope has been created.[1]

On this point Kierkegaard was sometimes contested by the
later "Theology of Hope." For it, the foundation of Christian

1. Søren Kierkegaard, *Works of Love*, Princeton University Press, 2013, Part II, nr. 3.

hope would not be the Incarnation ("the eternal that enters into time") but eschatology—that is, the Resurrection of Christ.[2] The first would make us fall back, it is believed, into the Greek idea of the "epiphany of the eternal in the present." The "Theology of Hope" brings a necessary integration to the previous perspective but does not make it obsolete. The two points of view must be kept together. At one point in history (the Incarnation), eternity has entered time; at another point in history (the Resurrection), time has entered eternity! The Christian horizon of eternity—as well as, more generally, the horizon of salvation—is made possible jointly by the Incarnation and Resurrection of Christ. Christmas is no less indispensable for Christian hope than Easter is. Other men have died and been resurrected according to the Bible, but they have not founded any new hope. If this happened with Christ, it is because his was not the death and resurrection of an ordinary person but that of a man-God. The universal meaning of Christ's death rests on the Incarnation. "The hope of Christianity is eternity, and Christ is the way; the lowering of him is the way, but even when he ascends to heaven he is the way."[3] The Incarnation and the Paschal Mystery together constitute the "way."

As long as we are in this world, however, eternity will always be in the future for us: "Although the eternal touches time, that is, it is in time, they do not meet in the present, since otherwise the present would be identified with eternity. . . . If therefore the eternal is in time, then it is in the future, that is, as a possibility."[4]

"Possibility" does not have an abstract meaning here, but a concrete existential meaning; it indicates what man is not yet but that he can, if he so wishes, become. Even more than the concept of nature, it can serve as a vehicle for biblical thought, since even for the Bible, human beings are not just what they are determined to be from their birth but also what they are called to become,

2. Jürgen Moltmann, *Theology of Hope*, London, 1967, Introduction.
3. Søren Kierkegaard, *Works of Love*, loc. cit.
4. Ibid.

through the exercise of their freedom, in obedience to the word of God. In other words, human beings are not only *nature* (a concept foreign to the Bible!) but also *vocation*.

Hope is by no means, as is often said, the virtue of young people. It is the virtue of all life and, perhaps, even more so of old age. As long as the word hope is used for all sorts of things, as it was before Christianity—that is, desire, nostalgia, the probability that something will happen or not—then certainly it is more natural in youth, when the possibilities are still many, while asking old people to give themselves up to hope "sounds almost as disrespectful as asking them to dress in the way of boys."

To understand what hope means for human life on earth, even more than its positive description, perhaps the negative one is useful: that is, looking at what existence becomes when eternity is ignored. Some of the best-known thinkers of the last century accepted the concept of possibility from Kierkegaard (as they accepted that of anguish, of the primacy of the single over the universal, and of existence over essence), while ignoring the horizon of faith in which he moved. Faith is what makes the difference between Kierkegaard and many of his "disciples." To him, faith is everything (Abraham, the man of faith, is his "hero"); for them, it is nothing and can easily be done without.[5]

The resulting picture constitutes, I believe, the best apology, in the negative, of Christian hope. What is—asked a well-known philosopher who also started from Kierkegaard—that "solid and certain core" to which conscience recalls us and on which our existence must be based if it is to be authentic? And the answer was: "The nothing!" All human possibilities are, in reality, impossibilities. Every attempt to plan and rise is a leap that starts from nothing and ends in nothing. Existential nullity does

5. Kierkegaard had foreseen his fate after death: "Always this infamous, ignoble cannibalism, with which (as Elagabalus ate ostrich brains) one devours the thoughts of the dead, their opinions, sayings, impressions. But for their life, their character: no, thank you, we don't want to have anything to do with all this" (*Journal*, X, 4 A, 537, year 1852).

not at all have the character of deprivation and deficiency with respect to an ideal proclaimed and not achieved. It is the being of this entity that is null prior to everything that can be planned and usually achieved. Planning itself is nothing.[6]

People need possibilities. They are like oxygen to them. Without them, they die of spiritual asphyxiation.

> Chance is the only thing that saves. When someone faints, they run in search of cologne, or Hoffmann's drops; but when someone wants to despair, you have to say: "Quick, find a chance for him, give him a chance!" Chance is the only remedy; give him a chance and the desperate man picks up his energy again and he revives, because if a person is left without a chance, it is as if he or she is out of air.[7]

The theological virtue of hope gives you something more than cologne and Hoffmann's drops. It tells you that God never leaves you without a chance, because his grace can make any situation, even the most desperate, an "opportunity for good." The biblical name for "possibility" is *kairòs*, a favorable occasion (2 Cor 6:2). If we look around us (or inside us!), we will soon discover the opportunity for good that is being offered to us at this very moment.

6. Martin Heidegger, *Being and Time*, §58.
7. Søren Kierkegaard, *The Sickness unto Death*, Part I, C.

22.
Get Up and Walk!

The door of the temple, called "the Beautiful Gate," is known for the miracle that occurred in front of it. A cripple lay there begging for alms. One day, Peter and John passed by, and we know what happened next. The cripple, healed, jumped to his feet and finally, after who knows how many years he had been lying there abandoned, he too went through that door and entered the temple "jumping and praising God" (Acts 3:1–9).

Something similar could also happen to us with regard to hope. We too often find ourselves, spiritually, in the position of the cripple on the threshold of the temple; inert and lukewarm, as if paralyzed in the face of difficulties. But here the divine hope passes by us, carried by the word of God, and says to us too, like Peter to the cripple and Jesus to the paralytic: "Get up and walk!" (Mk 2:11). And we jump to our feet and finally enter into the heart of the Church, ready to assume, again and joyfully, tasks and responsibilities. These are the daily miracles of hope. It is truly a great miracle worker; it puts thousands of cripples back on their feet, thousands of times. Indeed—as Isaiah told us—it puts eagle wings on their feet and makes people walk without stumbling.

What is extraordinary about hope is that its presence changes everything, even when externally nothing changes. I have a small example of this in my own life. I am a person who suffers from the cold much more than the heat. Now, in Italy, in March, at the beginning of spring, the temperature is more or less the same as in late October and early November. Yet I noticed that the cold of March made me less depressed than the cold of November. I wondered why and finally found the answer. The cold of November is a hopeless cold because we are heading toward winter. The cold of March is a cold with hope!

So far, we have tried to understand what hope is and what it means to hope. Now we would like to move on to practice and ask ourselves how to "keep hope alive," how to "account" for it, and how to "abound in hope" by virtue of the Holy Spirit. The Letter to the Hebrews compares hope to "an anchor of our life sure and firm." Sure and firm because it is cast not on earth but in heaven, not in time but in eternity, "beyond the veil of the sanctuary" (Heb 6:18–19). This image of hope has become classic. But we also have another image of hope, in a certain sense opposite to the previous one: the sail. If the anchor is what gives the boat safety and keeps it steady between the swaying of the sea, the sail is what makes it move and advance in the sea. Through both things does hope operate, both within the boat of the Church and our own lives. It is truly like a sail that collects the wind and without noise transforms it into a driving force that carries the boat, offshore or ashore according to the needs. Just as the sail in the hands of a good sailor is able to use any wind, from any direction, favorable or unfavorable, to move the boat in the desired direction, so does hope.

It is now a question of seeing how to orient this sail, how to use it so that it truly makes each of us advance toward holiness and helps the kingdom of God reach the ends of the earth. We are helped, even in this practical application, by the philosopher Kierkegaard, according to whom every truly Christian discourse must be "edifying."[1]

First of all, hope comes to our aid in our personal journey of *sanctification*. Hope becomes, in those who exercise it, the very

1. Cf. S. Kierkegaard, *The Gospel of Suffering*, IV.

principle of spiritual progress. Hope is always on guard to discover new "occasions for good," always something that can be done. Therefore, it does not allow them to settle down in lukewarmness and sloth. Hope is the complete opposite of what is sometimes thought; it is not a beautiful and poetic interior disposition that makes you dream and build imaginary worlds. On the contrary, it is very concrete and practical; it spends its time putting tasks to be done in front of you. When there is absolutely nothing to be done in a given situation, then, yes, it would be paralysis and despair. But hope, looking at eternity as it does, always finds that there is something that can be done to improve the situation: work harder, be more obedient, more humble, more mortified.

When you are tempted to say to yourself "There is nothing more to be done," hope comes forward and tells you "Pray!" You answer "But I prayed!" and she "Pray again!" And even when the situation should become extremely hard, such that it seems that there is really nothing more to be done, hope still points you to a task: to endure until the end and not lose patience. The Apostle, we have heard, recommends that we "abound in hope" but immediately adds how this becomes possible: not because of our efforts (we would not be able to) but "by virtue of the Holy Spirit."

Hope has a privileged relationship, in the New Testament, with patience. It is the opposite of impatience, of haste, of "everything, and now." It is the antidote to discouragement. It keeps the desire alive. It is also a great pedagogue in the sense that it does not point out everything at once—all there is to do or can be done—but puts in front of you one possibility at a time. She only gives "a daily bread." It distributes the effort and thus makes it possible to carry it out.

Scripture continually sheds light on this truth—that tribulation does not take away hope, but rather increases it: "Affliction produces endurance, and endurance, proven character, and proven character, hope" (Rom 5:3–4). Hope needs tribulation as the flame needs the wind to strengthen itself. Human reasons for hoping must die, one after another, for the true unshakable reason that is God to emerge. It happens as in the launch of a ship. It is necessary that the scaffolding that held the ship up artificially, when it was under construction, be removed and all the various props be taken away one after another so that it can take off and freely float on the water. Tribulation removes from us any "hold" and leads us to hope only in God. It leads to that state of perfection that consists in hoping when there seems to be no hope (Rom 4:18)—that is, to keep hoping by relying on the word once spoken by God, even when all human reasons for hoping have disappeared.

Such was Mary's hope under the cross. Apparently, Mary was "disappointed" in her hope. She had hoped until the very end that the error would be discovered, that her son's innocence would be recognized and that God would intervene. She hoped until they began stripping him to crucify him and even beyond that. Instead, nothing. Barabbas also had a mother and she too must have hoped for her son to be freed. Hope came true for her, not for Mary. But who would dare to say that Jesus' mother was "disappointed" by hope while Barabbas's mother was not? Theological hope is measured against the background of eternity, and we are witnesses that Mary was not disappointed for eternity.

Popular piety is not wrong when it invokes Mary with the title of *Mater Spei*, Mother of Hope. The Second Vatican Council points to her at the foot of the cross as the model not only of hope but of all three theological virtues and, on account of them, gives Mary the title of "Mother in the order of grace":

> She was united with Him by compassion as He died on the
> Cross. In this singular way she cooperated by her obedience,
> faith, hope and burning charity in the work of the Savior in

giving back supernatural life to souls. Wherefore she is our mother in the order of grace. (*Lumen Gentium*, 61)

23.
Ready to Account for Hope

In addition to our personal sanctification, theological hope is indispensable also for *evangelization*. In the First Letter of St. Peter, the spreading of the message is presented as "giving reason for hope": "Always be ready to give an explanation to anyone who asks you for a reason for your hope" (1 Pt 3:15–16). Reading what happened after Easter, one gets the feeling that the Church is born from a movement of hope. There is no other way of explaining the sudden transformation of the disciples and the enthusiasm for this virtue that shines through their writings. The Resurrection of Christ had truly "regenerated them to a living hope" (1 Pt 1:3), and with this hope, they set out to conquer the world.

Once again today, we need a regeneration of hope if we want to undertake a New Evangelization. Nothing is done without hope. People go where there is the scent of hope and flee where they do not feel its presence. Hope is what gives young people the courage to form a family or to follow a religious vocation; it is what keeps them away from drugs and other similar ways of surrendering to despair.

In a certain sense, compared to a few decades ago, we are today in a more advantageous situation with regard to hope. We no longer have to spend most of our time defending Christian hope from external attacks. We can therefore do the most useful and fruitful thing, which is to proclaim it, to offer it, and to spread it throughout the world, making ours a kerygmatic discourse on hope rather than an apologetic one.

Let's take a look at what has been happening with regard to Christian hope for over a century now. At first, there was a frontal attack on it by men such as Feuerbach, Marx, and Nietzsche. Christian hope was, in many cases, the direct target of their critique. Eternal life, the afterlife, and heaven: all such things were seen as the illusory projection of people's unsatisfied desires and needs in this world, a protest against our current misery, and, at the same time, opium that makes people fall asleep and distracts them from their historical tasks. According to the young Hegel, it was nothing else than "wasting in heaven the treasures destined for the earth."[1] Christians tried to defend the content of Christian hope, often with ill-concealed unease. Christian hope was "in the minority." We were almost afraid to talk about eternity.

But after having demolished Christian hope, the atheist Marxist culture did not take long to realize that human beings could not be left without hope. So, it invented "the Principle of hope."[2] With it, Marxist culture not only claimed to have demolished Christian hope but, worse still, to have gone beyond it and to be its legitimate heir—in short, to have discovered the true hope of which religious hope was just a naïve symbol. For the inventor of this "hope principle" (*principle*, mind you, no longer *virtue*), it is certain that hope is vital for humanity. It has a purpose which is "the revelation of the hidden man"—that is, of the still latent human possibilities.

Also, for Scripture there will be, in the future, the revelation of what we are now in a hidden way—that is, children of God (1 Jn 3:2); but here, we are dealing with a completely different kind of revelation. Christian hope is overturned. The manifestation of the Son of Man—that is, of Christ—is replaced by the

1. G.W.F. Hegel, *Frühe Schriften*, 1 (no. 34), in *Gesammelte Werke*, 1, Hamburg, 1989, p. 372.
2. Ernst Bloch, *Das Prinzip Hoffnung*, 3 vols., Berlin, 1954–1959.

manifestation of the hidden man; the *parousia* by *utopia*. Here, we see how the substitute for a truth can be worse than its denial, as putting oneself in the place of God is worse than denying God.

For a couple of decades, nothing was discussed more frequently in the theological faculties. Theologians rejoiced at the thought that there was someone on the other side of the divide who desired to take hope seriously and to establish a dialogue. The difference was so subtle and the language so similar! The heavenly homeland became the "homeland of identity"—not the place where man finally sees God face-to-face but where he sees the real man, in which perfect identity is achieved between what a human being *can be* and what he or she really *is*. The so-called "Theology of Hope" was born in response to this challenge. There were also fruitful discussions, but they were always marginal with respect to the real problem. The thing that is least perceptible in all these writings is precisely what St. Peter calls "living hope" (1 Pt 1:3), the thrill of hope.[3]

Now, I said, the situation has partly changed. The political collapse of Marxism, at least on the ideological level, has taken away much authority and relevance from these attacks on Christian hope. The task we have before us is no longer that of defending it and justifying it philosophically and theologically but—quite simply—that of announcing it, of showing it, and of giving it to a world that has lost the sense of hope and therefore is languishing spiritually. An ancient Father said:

> Take away hope and all humanity grows numb.
> Take away hope and all arts and virtues will fade away.
> Take away hope and everything perishes.[4]

3. To those who want to get an idea of what "living hope" is, I would suggest listening to some famous African American spirituals, for example "We Are Climbing Jacob's Ladder," sung by Paul Robeson in a famous concert of 1958.

4. Zeno of Verona, *Tractatus*, XXXVI, *De spe, fide et caritate*, I, 2 (CCL 22): "Tolle spem: torpet humanitas tota."

Hope is transmitted by contagion. It is not transmitted because one studies it, discusses it, or explains it, but only if one possesses it. As people upon leaving a church once used to pass blessed water from hand to hand, and at the beginning of the Easter Vigil the faithful lit their candles from those of others, so Christians must pass divine hope from parents to children.

If there is a means to infect others with hope, it is joy. Joy reveals the presence of hope like perfume does that of the flower.

24.
By the Virtue of the Holy Spirit

Let us recall the words of Paul mentioned above: "May the God of peace fill you with all joy and peace in faith, so that you may abound in hope by the virtue of the Holy Spirit" (Rom 15:13). In commenting on this *parenesis* on hope, we have come to the last word, the decisive one: the Holy Spirit. Hope is a theological virtue not only in the sense that it has God as its object and term but also because it has God at its origin. It is one of the forms, together with faith and charity, the action of the Holy Spirit takes when it comes to the soul. One of the "Three Graces"!

What St. Paul says about charity—that it is poured out into our hearts "through the Holy Spirit who has been given to us" (Rom 5:5)—applies to all three theological virtues. The relationship with the Holy Spirit is highlighted almost every time the three theological virtues are mentioned:

> For through the Spirit, by *faith*, we await the *hope* of righteousness. For in Christ Jesus, neither circumcision nor uncircumcision counts for anything, but only faith working through *charity*. (Gal 5:5–6)

It is the Holy Spirit who keeps our hope alive and helps us to exercise it, attesting to our spirit that we are children of God and, if children, also heirs (Rom 8:16–17). The historical foundation of hope is Christ and what he did with his death and Resurrection; but it is precisely this foundation that is made operative by the Holy Spirit. He is also the one who will one day fulfill our hope, making us rise with Christ. "If the Spirit of the one who raised Jesus from the dead dwells in you, the one who raised Christ from the dead will give life to your mortal bodies also, through his Spirit that dwells in you" (Rom 8:11).

Christian hope, like all things in the Church, needs to pass through a "bath of regeneration and renewal in the Holy Spirit" (Ti 3:5), to regain the strength of irradiation, to be freed from all the shackles that we have built around it like a too-complicated dress for a little girl who needs to move, to run, to be free to creep into the tightest places.

In the Bible, we find the echo of a great crisis of hope that leads all the people to exclaim: "Our hope is gone, we are lost" (Ez 37:11). It happened at the time of the exile. And how was this crisis overcome? God gave the prophet the vision of the withered bones and told him to cry out to the Spirit: "Spirit, come from the four winds, blow on these dead to revive them." The prophet prophesied and the bones got back on their feet and were a great army.

The Bible is dotted with such leaps of hope. One of them is described in the Third Lamentation, and it is too instructive not to dwell on it for a while. It is a word that the Church should make her own every time she finds herself at the bottom of a crisis. The prophet has before him the vision of Jerusalem reduced to rubble in the aftermath of its destruction. Corpses and ashes everywhere; enemies singing victory over it. To this is added the darkness of the soul: "I am the man who experienced misery under the whip of his anger." But here is the miracle worked by hope: suddenly, the prophet has an afterthought and says to himself:

But this I will call to mind;

therefore I will hope.

The Lord's acts of mercy are not exhausted,

his compassion is not spent.

They are renewed each morning. (Lam 3:21–23)

When the prophet decides to keep hoping, the tone changes completely: the lamentation turns into a heartfelt prayer for the restoration of the Holy City. In this spirit, it is recited by the Jews on the great day of fasting that commemorates the destruction of the temple, and the Church used to sing it, with poignant melody, in the Night Office of Holy Week, between the day of death and that of the Resurrection of Christ. Each time, what changes the situation is the decision or the cry: "I will hope!"

Christmas can be an occasion for us for one of these surges of hope. The poet we already know wrote (as we know by now, he let God himself speak):

Hope is a little, unassuming girl that came into the world on Christmas day last year.

. . .

Yet it is this small child who will cross worlds . . .

as the star has guided the three kings from the bottom of the East towards the cradle of my Son.[1]

If we want to give a name to this little girl, we can only call her Mary, the one who down here—says Dante, the other great poet of theological virtues—"among mortals" is "a living fountainhead of hope."[2]

---

1. Charles Péguy, *Le porche*, cit., p. 536.
2. *Paradise*, XXXIII, 12.

Part Three

I STAND AT THE DOOR
AND KNOCK

The Gate of Charity

25.
He Loved Us First

St. Zeno of Verona (300–371 AD), one of the most poetically gifted Latin Fathers, at a certain point in his treatise on the three theological virtues, shows us charity almost tired of hearing the praise of faith and hope, eager to "step forward" and assert her title of "queen of all virtues":

> May faith also triumph for all the qualities it wants and hope put forth its many and great merits; however both without charity will not stand. . . . Faith benefits only itself, charity everyone; faith does not fight without a reward, but charity wants to give even for nothing; faith does not pass into another, charity passes into a people; faith belongs to a few, charity to all; hope and faith have a limited time, charity has no end.[1]

But, as I said, it is only a poetic dramatization. Shortly before, the same author spoke, with equal fervor, of the "harmony" between the three virtues: "They appear so united to each other that one is indispensable to the other. In fact, if there is no hope, what does faith work for? If there is no faith, how will hope itself be born? If charity is removed from these, both will fail."[2] As in the image of the "Three Graces," each of the three theological virtues holds the other two by her hands.

The intimate link that binds the three theological virtues

1. Zeno of Verona, *De spe, fide et caritate*, cit., 4, 10.
2. Ibid., 1, 1.

together is expressed by the Apostle Paul in a text that we can consider a kind of biblical statute of the three theological virtues:

> Since we have been justified by *faith*,
> we have peace with God through our Lord Jesus Christ,
> through whom we have gained access [by faith] to this grace
> in which we stand, and we boast in *hope* of the glory of God . . .
> and hope does not disappoint,
> because the *love* of God has been poured out into our hearts
> through the holy Spirit that has been given to us. (Rom 5:1–5)

Love poured into our hearts—that is, the theological virtue of charity—is, at the same time, the love with which God loves us and with which he makes us love him and our neighbor.

We have come to the mother and nurse of all three theological virtues, at the door that leads into the most secret of rooms in the "interior castle." In the order of *generation*—that is, in the order in which they are manifested in us—faith and hope (logically, if not chronologically) precede charity because we cannot love what we do not know and do not hope for. In the order, however, of their *perfection*, writes St. Thomas Aquinas, "charity precedes faith and hope, since both are informed by charity and receive perfection as a virtue from it. In fact, charity is the mother and root of every virtue as it is the form of all virtues."[3]

The one who has most vigorously highlighted the excellence and superiority of charity is the Apostle Paul. In his famous hymn to charity in 1 Corinthians 13, he speaks of it as the "best way of all," superior to the manifestation of every charism of the Spirit, however spectacular, even performing miracles and speaking all languages. He makes charity "the fullness of the law," its summary and fulfillment (Rom 13:8–10). Faith will be replaced by vision and hope by possession: But what can love be replaced by?

---

3. *S. Th.*, I-IIae, q. 62, a. 4.

We must take all this for granted, however, and leave it aside to deal with something given less attention. Let us go back to our guiding image. What does it mean to open the door of love to God? Is it perhaps that we take the initiative to love God? This is how pagan philosophers would have replied according to their conception of the love of God. "God," says Aristotle, "moves the world insofar as he is loved."[4] (Insofar as he is loved, not insofar as he loves!) This view was completely reversed in the New Testament: "In this is love: not that we have loved God, but that he loved us. . . . We love because he first loved us" (1 Jn 4:10, 19).

What can we say (better, stammer) about this love "with which God loves us"? Every love is the movement of one being toward another being with the desire for union. The orientations of this movement, its modalities and its variants, are innumerable, but there is always a desire for union: either to possess the other or to donate oneself to the other. God's love for us is a movement toward us, not simply to be known by us or to be, in some way, imitated by us, but to be united with us and to give himself to us.

At times we read in the Bible that God loves some and abominates others, that "he hates all evildoers" (Ps 5:6). God had to speak in a human language, in a pedagogical way; but God hates evil, not the evildoer; the sin, not the sinner. In God's love, there is no "more" or "less." His love is pure quality, it has nothing quantitative: it is offered to everyone in its infinity. God does not *have* love, he *is* love! He can only love divinely—that is, giving all of himself.

God's love is similar to the atmospheric pressure that surrounds the earth, enwrapping every being and weighing on it. God "besieges" every person; he tries to open a breach, to find the path that leads to the heart and allows him to penetrate everywhere. The difference between the sinner and the saint, but also between one saint and another, lies in the fact of closing or

4. Aristotle, *Metaphysics*, XII, 7, 1072b: "The first motor [God] moves as object of love."

opening the heart to his love, of opening it a little or a lot. But it is always the same love, the same pressure, even though the mystery of the relationship between divine election and human freedom remains.

After receiving the revelation of the "excessive" love of God for us, all we can do is to say with the poet of the *Infinite*:

> And into this
> Immensity my thought sinks ever drowning,
> And it is sweet to shipwreck in such a sea. [5]

5

5. Giacomo Leopardi, *The Infinite* (trans. Henry Reed).

26.
We Have Believed in the Love of God!

Opening the door of love to Christ means a very specific thing: welcoming the love of God and believing in it. "We have come to know and to believe in the love God has for us" (1 Jn 4:16). Christmas is the manifestation, or the epiphany, of God's goodness and love for the world: "For the grace of God has appeared (*epephane*), saving all" (Ti 2:11). The most important thing to do at Christmas is to receive with amazement the infinite gift of God's love.

When you receive a gift, it is not courteous to present your gift immediately with the other hand, perhaps already prepared in advance. One inevitably gives the impression of wanting to pay it back immediately. It is necessary first to honor the gift received and its donor with amazement and gratitude. Then, almost ashamed and with modesty, one can give one's own gift, as if it were nothing compared to what one has received. (In reality, our gift to God is less than nothing!) The most beautiful thing we can do for God at Christmas is not to look for what to offer God in return but to forget everything, to be enchanted and to be in awe in front of his infinite love. In a word, to believe in God's love for us!

It seems like an easy thing to do; instead, it is among the hardest things in the world. We are more inclined to be active than passive, to do rather than to let ourselves be done to.

Unconsciously, we do not want to be debtors but creditors; we want God's love as a reward rather than as a gift. In this way, however, a shift and an overturning are taking place: duty is put above gift, law above grace, works above faith, and human "good will" above God's benevolence.

A revealing fact of this tendency is precisely the way in which, for centuries, the Greek phrase of Luke 2:14 was translated in the *Gloria* of the Mass and in Christian language: *Pax hominibus bonae voluntatis*: "Peace on earth to men of goodwill." One could, *per se*, keep this traditional translation (as we are obliged to do when the *Gloria* is recited or sung in Latin), provided however that by "the goodwill" (*eudokia* in Greek) we mean the benevolence of God toward men, as in Ephesians 1:9, not the human goodwill toward God or among themselves. This is how the expression is rendered nowadays in the main Western languages.[1] I hope that this is also the sense intended in the new translation of the English Missal—"And on earth peace to people of goodwill"—otherwise, something very important (and comforting!) of the original Gospel proclamation would be lost.[2]

There are treatises on the duty and the degrees of God's love—in other words, on the God who must be loved (*De diligendo Deo*). I know of no treatises on the God who loves! True, the Bible is itself a treatise on the God who loves, but almost always, despite this, when people speak of "the love of God," God is the object, not the subject of the sentence. Now, it is true that to love God with all one's strength is "the first and greatest commandment." This is certainly the first thing in the order of the commandments; but the very order of the commandments is not the first order. Before the order of the commandments, there is

1. Spanish: "En la tierra paz a los ombres que ama el Señor"; Italian: "Pace in terra agli uomini amati dal Signore"; French: "Paix sur la terre aux hommes qu'il aime"; German: "Friede auf Erden den Menschen seiner Gnade."

2. Nothing prevents us from keeping in honor the traditional expression "people of goodwill" in its anthropological meaning, so common nowadays in the Church-world dialogue, without blurring, however, its original theological significance in the liturgy.

the order of grace—that is, of God's gratuitous love. The commandment itself is founded on the gift; the duty to love God is based on being loved by God: "We love because he first loved us." This is the novelty of the Christian faith with respect to any philosophical or religious ethics based on "duty" or on the "categorical imperative." We should never lose sight of it.

This then, I repeat, is what it means to open the door of love to Christ: to open yourself to the experience of God's love, not to be afraid, and to allow yourself to be "evangelized"—that is, to be permeated and inflamed by the beautiful and joyful news that God loves you and sent his Son to convince you of this: "In this way the love of God was revealed to us: God sent his only Son into the world so that we might have life through him" (1 Jn 4:9).

"We believe in God's love for us!" This is a cry for which we must gather all our strength. I call it "unbelieving faith": faith that cannot be persuaded of what it believes, even if it does believe it. Faith with wonder! God—the Eternal, the Being, and the All—loves me and takes care of me, a little nothing lost in the immensity of the universe and of history!

You have to become a child to believe in love. Children believe in love. Oh, how they believe in it! Not, however, on the basis of some reasoning, but rather by instinct, by nature. They are born full of confidence in the love of their parents. They can later on be disappointed and become mistrustful because the parents are not God and they can fall short. Children ask their parents for the things they need, even stamping their feet, but the unspoken assumption is not that they have earned it, but rather that they are the children and that one day they will be the heirs of everything. Children are not afraid of love. They wallow in it. The more you give them, the more they take.

But it is not easy to become a child again. Experiences, the bitterness and the disappointments of life, all this makes us cautious, sometimes cynical, even if we desperately need to open our hearts to God's love. We are all a little like Nicodemus. "How can a person once grown old be born again?" (Jn 3:4). How can we be reborn, get excited again, and be amazed at Christmas as children are? What did Jesus answer Nicodemus? "Amen, amen, I say to you, no one can enter the kingdom of God without being born of water and Spirit" (Jn 3:5).

This is not the result of human effort and ambition or an excitement of the heart; it is the work of the Holy Spirit. Jesus does not speak here only of baptism, at least not just water baptism. It is a question of a rebirth and a baptism in the Spirit, or "from above" (Jn 3:3), which can be renewed several times in the course of one's life. Do we desire it? St. Bonaventure concludes his *Journey of the Mind to God* with these allusive words:

> No one knows this mystical and most hidden wisdom, except one who receives it. And no one receives it except one who desires it. And no one desires it but one who is set on fire internally by the fire of the Holy Spirit, whom Christ has sent into the world.[3]

---

3. Bonaventure, *Itinerarium mentis in Deum*, VII, 4.

27.

God as Absolute Love

Henri de Lubac wrote: "The world must know: the revelation of Love upsets everything it had conceived of the divinity."[1] To this day we have not yet finished (and never will) drawing all the consequences from the evangelical revolution about God as love. With the help of the Holy Spirit, who does not cease guiding the Church "to the full truth," let us try to understand what is, concerning the theological virtue of charity, the consequence still to be discovered, and above all to be lived.

In past times, the theological discourse on God started from the definition of God as "absolute being" (*ens a se*). This was based on the name of God revealed to Moses in the episode of the burning bush—"I am who I am" (Ex 3:14)—and also on the expression "I am" with which God presents himself in Isaiah (Is 45:3). Today we know that the original Hebrew sense of the expression is more existential than essential; it affirms that God exists, that he is a God present and active in history, rather than explaining what God is in himself. It must therefore be translated as "I am there" or "I exist for you."[2]

Since we set out to also value the modern, existential point of view on the theological virtues, we must take into account that the New Testament offers us a different starting point for speaking of God, that of God as "absolute love." This is a starting point that is not an alternative to the metaphysical one but is

1. Henri de Lubac, *Histoire et Esprit*, Aubier, Paris 1950, chap. V.
2. Gerhard von Rad, *Old Testament Theology*, vol. 1, part II, chap. 3, SCM Press, 2012.

more significant for people of today and above all more biblical, for it is written that "God is love [*agàpe*]" (1 Jn 4:8). St. Gregory Nazianzen defines God as "an ocean of being [*ousia*] without limits"[3]; we can add "an ocean of love without limits." For God, to be is to love.

"God is love" is a universal statement, but abstract and timeless—a nominal predicate; it becomes concrete and affecting human history—a verbal predicate—in Jesus' phrase "God so loved [*egàpesen*] the world that he gave his only Son" (Jn 3:16). The whole Bible—observes St. Augustine—"does nothing but narrate the love of God."[4]

One might ask: Why do we give so much importance to the concept of love, distinguishing it from any other? Is it not also written, for example, and by John himself, that "God is light" (1 Jn 1:5)? The reason is that light is a physical phenomenon and can be attributed to God only metaphorically, while love belongs to the spiritual world and is said of God properly. Love is the same thing in God and in us; only its quality is infinitely different.

In the philosophical and religious currents of the time (Platonism, Stoicism, Hermetic literature, Philo of Alexandria), we encounter various concepts and symbols of God present in the Gospel of John, such as Logos, light, and life; what is totally absent in them is the concept of love as understood in the New Testament. In the novel *Quo Vadis*, a pagan asks the Apostle Peter, who had just arrived in Rome: Athens has given us wisdom, Rome power; what does your religion offer us? And Peter replies, "Love"![5] The author of the novel has hit the mark.

"If God is not love, then God does not exist at all!"[6] We cannot unreservedly adhere to this affirmation of our friend

3. Gregory Nazianzen, *Oratio*, 45, 3 (PG 36, 625).

4. Augustine, *De catechizandis rudibus*, I, 8, 4 (PL 40, 319).

5. Henryk Sienkiewicz, *Quo Vadis*, chap. 33.

6. See Søren Kierkegaard, *The Gospel of Suffering*, IV. The splendid Kierkegaardian vision of God as love is partly weakened by his silence on the intra-Trinitarian love that is the foundation of every expression of God's love.

Kierkegaard (justice is also a precious value for us humans!); but it contains something profoundly true and liberating. The history of religions (Babylonian, Etruscan, Aztec, but also primitive religions still practiced) show us what the idea of a God who is anything but love produces: a God to whom people must continually offer sacrifices, even of human hearts, to placate his wrath and obtain his favors.

Better to have no God at all than to have a hostile God! Humanity, even nonbelievers, will never be grateful enough to the Bible for this purification of God's image. Grateful, in particular, to Christ who freed the biblical religion itself from elements of that archaic idea of God that had crept into it from the environment in which it was born. Jesus has forever broken the alliance between violence and the sacred.[7] He did not offer victims, but he offered himself as a victim; he did not come with the blood of others, but with his own blood (Heb 9:12–14).

The God of Jesus Christ is a "friendly" God, indeed a *philanthropist*, according to St. Paul (Ti 3:4)!

---

7. René Girard, *Things Hidden Since the Foundation of the World*, Stanford University Press, 1978.

28.
Why the Trinity?

In the next few chapters, I will try to show how the main mysteries of the Christian faith—the Trinity, the Incarnation, and the Passion of Christ—start to shine with new light when we move with the vision of God as love.

First of all, the Trinity. The philosopher Kant has written that "the doctrine of the Trinity, taken literally, has no practical relevance at all."[1] He was speaking from a strictly philosophical point of view, and the Trinity—a "metaphysical" poet has written—is "bones to philosophy, but milk to faith."[2] Nevertheless, his statement has had negative effects on Western theology. If the doctrine of a triune God—rather than the Enlightenment idea of a vague "Supreme Being"—had been more alive in the Church, Ludwig Feuerbach could not so easily have spread his thesis, according to which God is a projection that man makes of his own essence, and it is he, man, who made God in his image, not the contrary. This theory doesn't apply, in fact, to the Christian God. What need would people have to divide their essence into three—Father, Son, and Spirit?

On several occasions I have preached the Word of God to Christians who live in countries with a Muslim majority where, however, there is a relative tolerance and the possibility of dialogue, as in the United Arab Emirates. Those Christians, mostly immigrants and employed as laborers, have sometimes asked me

1. Immanuel Kant, *Conflict of the Faculties*, Appendix II, 1, a (University of Nebraska Press, 1979), p. 65.

2. John Donne, *A Litany, 4: The Trinity.*

to help them answer a question they are often asked at their work-place: "Why do you Christians say you are monotheists if you do not believe in only one God?"

This is how I advised them to respond and how we ourselves should respond to those among us who ask the same question. We Christians believe in a triune God because we believe that God is love. God is love: therefore, he is Trinity! All love is love of someone or something; there is no "empty" love, without an object, just as there is no knowledge that is not knowledge of someone or something. Now, whom does God love to be called love? The universe? Humankind? But then he has only been love for some billions of years—that is, since the physical universe has existed. Before that, whom did God love to be called love, since God cannot change and begin to be what he was not before?

The Greek thinkers, conceiving of God above all as Intelligence (*Nous*), could answer: God thought of himself; he was "pure thinking."[3] But this is no longer possible when it is said that God is love, because "pure love of oneself" would be self-ishness, which is not the highest exaltation of love but its total contradiction. Here is the answer of revelation, which was dog-matically defined at Nicaea in 325. God has always been love, *ab aeterno*, because even before there was an object outside him to love, he had in himself the Word, the "only begotten Son," whom he loved with infinite love—that is, "in the Holy Spirit."

Goethe's Faust ponders possible alternatives to the incipit of St. John's prologue: Should we say that "In the beginning was the Thought (*der Sinn*)"? Or that "In the beginning was the Energy (*die Kraft*)"? No, he triumphantly concludes, "In the beginning was the Action (*die Tat*)!" The most important and the truest statement is missing: "In the beginning was Love!" The simple existence of another person "beside God," before the creation of the world, is the strongest proof that God is a communion of

3. Aristotle, *Metaphysics*, XII, 7, 1072b.

love. True, the word comes from the thought, but this Word is, first of all, a Son, and every son is born from love, especially this Son whom the Scripture literally calls "the Son of [the Father's] love" (Col 1:13). The Father's "Thought" is, of course, equally involved in the process, for love presupposes knowledge. No danger of falling back into a blind voluntarism!

All this does not explain *how* unity can be trinity at the same time, a mystery unknowable to us because it occurs only in God. However, it helps us to understand *why*, in God, unity must also be communion and plurality. A God who was pure knowledge or pure law, or absolute power, would not need to be triune. This would actually complicate things. No triumvirate and no diarchy have ever lasted long in history!

Christians, too, are monotheists and believe in the unity of God: a unity, however, not mathematical and numerical but of love and communion. The problem, if anything, is to know whence to start our discourse on God: whether from unity or from the Trinity. St. Gregory Nazianzen left a famous description of the path followed by God in revealing to us the mystery of the Trinity:

> The Old Testament explicitly announced the existence of the Father, while the existence of the Son was announced more obscurely. The New Testament manifested the existence of the Son, while it gave a glimpse of the divine nature of the Holy Spirit. Now the Spirit is present in our midst and grants us his manifestation more distinctly. It would not have been convenient, when the divinity of the Father had not yet been confessed, to openly proclaim that of the Son, nor would it have been safe to place upon us the weight of the divinity of the Spirit when that of the Son had not yet been accepted.[4]

4. Gregory Nazianzen, *Oratio*, 31. An ambiguity should be noted in the text. The Father who revealed himself in the Hebrew Testament, is not yet "the Father of our Lord Jesus Christ," that is, a true father of a true son. He is not the God Father in the Trinity, but father in the

We live, then, in a time when the Trinity has fully revealed itself; but what about the unbelieving, secularized world around us? Is it not in the same condition as humanity before the coming of Christ? Should we not use, then, the same pedagogy that God used in revealing himself in the history? We, too, must help our contemporaries to discover, first of all, that God exists, that he created us out of love, that he is a merciful father, not a cold and impersonal "supreme being." In short, that he is the God revealed by Jesus Christ!

You do not come to knowledge of the Trinity through human speculation, and if you do arrive, as Hegel did, it is no longer a trinity of living persons, but a trinity of ideas—thesis, antithesis, and synthesis, a poor product of human mind. We come to the knowledge of the Trinity through the same way by which the Trinity chose to reveal itself to us: "No one knows the Father except the Son and anyone to whom the Son wishes to reveal him" (Mt 11:27).

---

metaphorical sense of "the father of his people Israel," as for the pagans he was "the father of the cosmos." Jesus highlights the difference between the two fatherhoods, calling God "my Father and your Father" (Jn 20:17). The true God Father is only revealed by the coming of the Son.

29.
How to Speak of the Trinity Today

The inadequacy of our human language never does so painfully appear as when we talk about the Trinity. Apart from the Holy Spirit, which in Greek is a neutral term (and in some Semitic languages even a feminine term), the names Father and Son are inevitably marked by the gender limitation, while in God there is no distinction of sex. If it were possible (but it is certainly not), "inclusive" names could be coined that are equivalent to father/mother for the first divine person and son/daughter for the second person. What can be done, instead, is to remind ourselves and the faithful that God the Father in reality is father and mother (as the Bible oft suggests) and the second divine person, in his eternal generation, is son and daughter, firstborn among many brothers and firstborn among many sisters.

At the time when the Trinitarian dogma was being formulated, people—we know from the historical sources—excitedly discussed the Trinity even in the squares and at the market. That is certainly not the case anymore. We must find a way to proclaim the mystery of the triune God using categories that are meaningful and understandable today. It is not easy to present to modern people the Trinitarian mystery in terms of substance and hypostasis, nature and persons, used by the Fathers, even if the Church can never give up using them in the context of her theology and liturgy.

We speak of three "persons" in the Trinity: Father, Son, and Holy Spirit. However, the term person is inadequate to express what the Father and the Son are and even less what the Holy Spirit is. St. Augustine already noted that we use the term "person" in the absence of something better, "so as not to remain completely silent."[1] We also use it because, in the human sphere, the term person indicates what is most noble in the realm of the spirit.

It's easy for us to speak of the Son as a person, because he became incarnate, took on our nature, and continues to be God and man "in one person." We can get an idea of the Father as a person by analogy with the human person of the father. But how can we apply the term person to the Holy Spirit? He is not a concrete entity, and in the Bible, we find only images and symbols that express his functions: the wind (from which his Hebrew name, *Ruah*, derives), the dove, the fire, and the perfume. Paraclete itself stands for a function, that of advocate and counselor.

An analogy can help us. In the natural realm, we see the person who loves and we see the person who is loved, but we do not see the love that circulates between the two. Between two human people, love is a feeling that can grow, decrease, and end; in the Trinity, it is so real, immutable, and objective that it constitutes what Latin theologians call a "subsistent relationship," and the Greek, a "hypostasis." The New Testament uses an image more within our reach: that of the "seal."[2] We can also think of the ring that spouses exchange. They are all poor human attempts, but all we have is these.

Someone has proposed that we should continue using the term "person" for the Holy Spirit; not, though, as "the third person singular" of the Trinity but as "the first plural person"! The Holy Spirit would be the "We" of the Father and the Son, the

1. Augustine, *De Trinitate*, VII, 6, 11.
2. On the Holy Spirit as a "Seal" (*Sphragis*), see Jn 6:27; 2 Cor 1:22; Eph 1:13; Basil of Caesarea, *De Spiritu Sancto*, 64 (PG 32, 185).

love that unites them.[3] In this sense, the Trinity is not declined in "I—You—He" but in "I—You—We." Imagining, as poor mortals, the Father and the Son speaking between them of the Holy Spirit: they would not say "He" but "We."

There are no human categories that can help us talk about the Holy Spirit. All the analogies are inadequate. One thinks, for example, of a child being born: it is the fruit of both the love of the father and the mother; in its heart, there is the sum of these two loves, it unites them, reciprocates them; love circulates among the three, each in a different role as father, mother, and child. The child, however, comes to existence after its parents and can live independently from them: something that cannot be applied to the Holy Spirit.

In conclusion, we can and must continue to call the Holy Spirit "the third person" of the Trinity, as Tradition teaches us and all Christian Churches do, for only in this way do we understand that he has his own role. Father, Son, and Holy Spirit are all three one; only the mutual relationships are different,[4] and the relationship of the Spirit consists precisely in being the love that passes between the Father and the Son.

Far from being an "appendix" in the Trinity, the Holy Spirit is its very heart! According to the best Latin pneumatology, his proper name is not however "Holy Spirit" (both Father and Son are equally holy and are spirit!); his distinctive and "personal" name is rather Gift (*Donum*). In the Trinity, he is the mutual self-giving of the Father and the Son personified; in the history of salvation, he is the gift Father and Son make of themselves to believers in Christ, that we call "grace."[5] Being the mutual gift of the Father and the Son, the Holy Spirit is also their mutual joy

---

3. Heribert Mühlen, *Der Heilige Geist als Person: Ich—Du—Wir*, Münich, 1963.

4. See the axiom of St. Anselm of Canterbury, sanctioned by the Council of Florence (DS, 1330): "In Deo omnia sunt unum, ubi non obviat relationis oppositio": "In God everything is in common except what pertains to the relationship of each person."

5. Augustine, *De Trinitate*, XV, 18, 32; Thomas Aquinas, *S. Th.*, I, q. 38, a. 2.

and happiness. St. Augustine has written some stupendous words on this subject: "The inexpressible embrace . . . of the Father and the Image is not without enjoyment, without charity, without happiness. So this love, delight, felicity or blessedness—if any human word can be found that is good enough to express it—that Hilary calls enjoyment (*fruitio*), is the Holy Spirit in the triad, not begotten, but the sweetness of begetter and begotten pervading all creatures according to their capacity."[6]

The Holy Spirit is the "air" and the "perfume" we will breathe up there, the joyful embrace in which we will be included for eternity! Pious imagination? Wishful thinking? No, a pale reflection of the reality, like a sky painted on a sheet of paper compared to the true sky!

Classical theology has created an alternative to the term "persons" for the Trinity, that of "subsistent relationships" we have just mentioned.[7] To say that Father, Son, and Holy Spirit are subsistent relations means that the person does not *have* a relation; rather, he *is* that relation. A human person, besides being a father, is also someone's son, a woman's husband, a businessman, and so on; he is not limited to being a father. God the Father exists only insofar as he is the Father of the Son whom he generates "in the Holy Spirit."[8]

When circumstances and the interest of the audience allow it, we can refer to this concept of person as relation when speaking of the Trinity. We are encouraged to do this by the evolution the term person underwent in modern times. Person is no longer seen as an "individual" closed and complete in itself, but as an "I" who becomes aware of himself or herself in the presence of a "you." In other terms, as "a being-in-relation" or "being-in-communion." It was precisely the Christian doctrine of the Trinity that made this modern evolution possible by defining the divine persons as

6. Augustine, *De Trinitate*, VI, 2, 11; see Hilary of Poitiers, *De Trinitate*, II, 1.

7. Thomas Aquinas, *S. Th.*, I, q. 29, a. 4.

8. On this topic, see Excursus 2 at the end of this book.

pure relationships.[9] The modern concept of person as relation is more suited for the Father, the Son, and the Holy Spirit than the ancient one of individual or hypostasis.

If there is something capable of helping modern people to get some understanding of the Trinity, this, I repeat, is precisely love. God is "pure act," and this act is an act of love involving, simultaneously and *ab aeterno*, a lover, a loved one, and the love that unites them.[10] The mystery of mysteries is not, after all, the Trinity; it's rather to understand what love truly is. We can say it is "the good as self-diffusive" (*bonum diffusivum sui*) of Scholasticism, provided we give the adjective the same importance as the noun and make subject and predicate interchangeable. In other words, love is the free, gratuitous, and joyful self-giving and self-diffusing of the good. It begins in the Trinity with the generation of the Son, and in an essentially different way, it continues in creation and finds its culmination (*telos*) in the death of Christ.

We know the love "which unfolds throughout the universe": pages—indeed, less than words and syllables—which are detached from a single "bound volume" which is God himself.[11] Since love is the very essence of God, we will not be given to fully comprehend what it is (in reality and not just in definition!), not even in eternal life. Something better than knowing it, however, shall be given to us—namely, possessing it and being satiated with it eternally. You cannot embrace the ocean, but you can dive into it!

9. Cf. John Zizioulas, *Being as Communion: Studies in Personhood and the Church*, London, 1985.

10. The so-called "mysticism of the essence" urges the soul to go beyond even the category of love, which supposes the duality of lover and loved one, in order to stick to the category of being and essence, which is pure unity. This is the weak point of any theological system that—in line with the Neoplatonic "One" of Proclus—places the divine nature at the beginning and at the center of the discourse on God, instead of the person of God the Father. What remains in the shadows, in this case, is the radical novelty of Christian mysticism—Christological and Trinitarian—compared to other mystical traditions (or even philosophical systems) in which the very idea of a personal God is missing.

11. Dante Alighieri, *Paradise*, XXXIII, 85–87: "I saw that in its depth far down is lying / Bound up with love together in one volume, / What through the universe in leaves is scattered" (trans. Longfellow).

30.
Why the Incarnation?

Let us start this chapter with the famous question of St. Anselm of Canterbury (1033–1109): *Cur Deus homo?*—"Why did God become man?" Apparently, St. Augustine had already given a precise answer to this question: "Love pushed him to take our flesh"[1]; but Anselm poses the problem from the broader point of view of the entire history of salvation; moreover he wants to provide an answer based on reason, not just on faith.

We know his solution. It is because only someone who was, at the same time, man and God could redeem us from sin. As a man, in fact, he could represent all of humanity, and being God, what he did had an infinite value, proportionate to the debt that humankind had contracted with God the Father by sinning.

This answer is shared by Byzantine theology. The situation— wrote Nicholas Cabasilas (1322–1392)—was the following: man had to fight Satan and pay the debt of sin. He could not do it, however, being a slave to the one he needed to defeat, and the debt he owned being infinite. God, for his part, could win, but he didn't have to fight, since he was not the debtor. "This is why," he continues, "it was necessary that the one and the other were united and the two natures became one single person. In this way the one who had to fight was the same who could win."[2]

The answer of St. Anselm and Cabasilas is perennially valid, but it is not the only answer, nor is it an entirely satisfactory one.

---

1. Augustine, *In Ioh.*, 6, 13: "Caritas ergo illum adduxit ad carnem."
2. Nicolas Cabasilas, *Vita in Christo*, I, 5 (PG 150, 513).

In the creed, we profess that the Son of God became flesh "for us men and for our salvation," but our salvation is not limited to the remission of sins alone, much less of a particular sin, the original one. There remains room, therefore, for a deepening of the faith.

This is what Duns Scotus (1265–1308) tried to do. God, he says, became man because this was the original divine plan, prior to the fall itself—namely, that the world, created "through Christ and for him" (Col 1:16), should find in him, "in the fullness of time," its crowning and its recapitulation (Eph 1:10).[3] "First of all," Scotus writes, "God loves himself"; then, he "wants to be loved by someone who loves him in the highest possible degree outside of himself"; therefore, he "foresees the union with the nature that had to love him in the highest degree." This perfect lover could not be any creature, being finite, but only the eternal Word, who, therefore, would become incarnate "even if no one had sinned."[4] Adam's sin determined the modality of the Incarnation (atonement through Passion and death), not the fact itself. This was not a new idea in theology, even if it was a forgotten one. For Irenaeus and Athanasius, the Incarnate Word is the one in whose image man, before his sin, was created.[5] Before both of them, Scripture had said the same: "He chose us in him [Christ], before the foundation of the world" (Eph 1:4).

Unfortunately, however, at the beginning of everything there is still in Scotus (as in Aristotle!) a God to be loved, not a God who loves. This is due to the fact that the starting point of every discourse on the Trinity, in line with the Western vision, is the divine nature—God as "infinite Being" (*Ens infinitum*)—not the person of the Father. And a *nature*, unlike the *person*, is not a subject capable of loving! (On this point, our Orthodox brothers,

---

3. Teilhard de Chardin's theory of Christ as the "Omega point" of the evolution of the universe was inspired by the same biblical vision of Scotus, although from a more scientific than theological point of view.

4. Duns Scotus, *Opus Parisiense*, III, d. 7, q. 4 (*Opera omnia*, XXIII, Paris, 1894, p. 303).

5. Irenaeus of Lyon, *Adversus Haereses*, V, 16, 2; Athanasius, *De Incarnatione*, 13; *Contra Arianos*, 3, 10.

heirs of the Greek Fathers, have followed a better path than we Latins.)

Scripture calls us to take a step forward in regard to Scotus, always aware, however, that our affirmations about God are nothing but fleeting finger marks on the surface of the ocean. God the Father decides the Incarnation of the Word not because he wants to have someone outside himself *to be loved by* in a way worthy of him, but because he wants to have someone outside himself *to love* in a way worthy of him! Not to receive love, but to pour it out. Presenting Jesus to the world, in Baptism and in the Transfiguration, the heavenly Father says: "This is my *beloved* Son" (Mk 1:11; 9:7); he does not say "my *loving* Son."

At the origin of this vision there is the dazzling intuition of St. Augustine and the school born from him.[6] As we have already mentioned, speaking of the Trinity, they define the Father as the lover, the Son as the beloved, and the Holy Spirit as the love that unites them. On this point, we Latins too have something precious—and in my opinion equally essential—to offer, in view of an ecumenical synthesis. A full reconciliation between the two theologies, Eastern and Western, no longer appears so difficult and remote and it would be a decisive step toward the unity of the Church.

Only the Father, in the Trinity (and in the whole universe!), does not need to be loved to exist; he only needs to love.[7] The Son exists thanks to the Father; the Father exists thanks to no one. This is what guarantees the role of the Father as the unique source and origin of the Trinity while assuring the equality in nature of the three divine persons—that is, their common sharing in the "absolute love." Love is the reason for both the trinity and

6. Augustine, *De Trinitate*, VIII, 9,14; IX, 2, 2; XV, 17, 31; Richard of St. Victor, *De Trin.*, III, 2.18; Bonaventure, *I Sent.*, d. 13, q.1.

7. In this context we can find the only possible explanation of the saying of Jesus "The Father is greater than I" (Jn 14:28) that is not in contrast with his other affirmation: "The Father and I are one" (Jn 10:30).

the unity of God. It allows God to be "unique," without being "alone" and solitary. The Scholastic distinction between the unity of God (*De Deo Uno*) and the Trinity (*De Deo Trino*) may have a historical and practical justification, but it can be misleading because the "one God" of Christians is the Trinity!

The first movement of love is therefore *agape*, not *eros*, even if the two movements of love are inseparable (we will explain why later). It is the same reason (if we can speak, in this case, of a "reason") for which the Father generates the Son in eternity—that is, to give him his love, even before (here, however, there is no "before"!) wanting to be loved by him.

This is also the reason why God created the world! To the question "Why did God create us?" the catechism we learned as children taught us to answer: "To know him, love him and serve him in this life and then enjoy him in eternal life." Right answer, but incomplete! It explains the *purpose*, not the *cause* of creation; it says what the final cause is, not what the efficient cause is. It answers the question "For what purpose did God create us?"; it does not answer the most important question: "What prompted him to create us?" In fact, this question cannot be answered by "so that we love him," but by "because he loved us." To give, not to receive! In God, *eros* itself is *agape*! He desires and seeks to be loved by his creatures, but for their good, not for his benefit. "God," St. Irenaeus writes, "did not seek friendship with Abraham because of his need, but because, being good, he wanted to give Abraham eternal life. . . . Thus, in the beginning, God did not create Adam because he needed man, but to have someone on whom to pour down his benefits."[8]

What should we conclude from this overview on the question of Adam's sin and the Incarnation? That *a world with sin and with Jesus* is better than *a world without sin and without Jesus*! In a moment of inspired enthusiasm, this is what the Latin Church

8. Irenaeus of Lyon, *Adversus Haereses*, IV, 13, 4–14, 2.

dared to sing, before the outbreak of the anti-Pelagian controversy led theology to an obsessive and unilateral concentration
on sin and human corruption. In the Easter *Exsultet*, the liturgy
exclaims: "O happy fault [of Adam] that has procured for us such
and so great a Redeemer!"[9]

The Bible teaches us that God had thought of an even better
possibility—the one highlighted by Scotus—which sin prevented
from being realized, namely, *a world without sin and with Jesus.*
But then, would we have known how far God's love and mercy
can go? This is the first and the fundamental realization of the
principle that God can often bring good even from evil: "Where
sin increased, grace overflowed all the more" (Rom 5:20).[10]

St. Anselm's famous exclamation "You did not realize yet the
full weight of sin"[11] needs to be followed by another exclamation:
"We have not realized yet the full splendor of Christ's grace!" "The
only entrance door to Christianity" is not "the consciousness of
sin," as our friend Kierkegaard has written,[12] but the discovery of
the person of Jesus Christ.

---

9. "O felix culpa, quae talem ac tantum meruit habere Redemptorem!" On this point, the
Exsultet repeats, almost literally, what St. Ambrose of Milan had written in his work *In Psalmum*
(39, 20): "Happy [Adam's] fault that led to something better" ("Felix ruina, quae reparatur in
melius"); *Institutio Virginis*, 17, 104: "Adam's sin benefited us more than it harmed us" ("Am-
plius nobis profuit culpa, quam nocuit.")

10. See Augustine, *De correptione et gratia*, 9, 24, from which the famous expression
"etiam peccata," often attributed to him, is derived.

11. Anselm of Canterbury, *Cur Deus homo*, I, 21: "Nondum considerasti quanti ponderis
sit peccatum."

12. Søren Kierkegaard, *Practice in Christianity*, I, Moral. This should not make us forget
that, precisely on the discovery of the mystery of Christ (the "Paradox"), the author has written—in this same work—some of the most profound and touching words that human intelligence has ever dared to say about him.

31.
Why the Passion?

The vision of God as love, which illuminates our way of under-standing the Trinity, creation, and the Incarnation, sheds its light also on the Paschal Mystery. It does not only answer the question "Why did God become man?" but also the question "Why did God suffer on the cross?"

"By his wounds you have been healed." With these words, spoken of the Servant of Yahweh (Is 53:5–6), the faith of the Church has expressed the saving meaning of Christ's death (1 Pt 2:24). But can wounds, cross, and pain—negative facts and, as such, only deprivations of good—produce such a positive re-ality, which is the salvation of all mankind? The truth is that we have not been saved by Christ's suffering but by his love! More precisely, by the love that is expressed in the sacrifice of oneself.

At the time of St. Bernard, there was already someone who found the idea of a God "pleased" in the death of his Son to be repugnant. The saint replied to him: "It was not his death that pleased God but his will to die spontaneously. . . . God the Father did not ask for the blood of his Son, he accepted it as an offer-ing."[1] St. Bernard was simply commenting on Jesus' words: "This is why the Father loves me, because I lay down my life in order to take it up again. No one takes it from me, but I lay it down on my own" (Jn 10:17).

In many languages, the word "passion" serves to express two things—namely, a great love or a great pain. Love is the fire

1. Bernard of Clairvaux, *Contra errores Abelardi*, VIII, 21–22.

that Jesus came to bring to earth; in his Passion (his "baptism"), this fire destroyed the sin of the world, like quicklime pulverizes the stone thrown into it. Christ's pain retains all its value, and the Church will never cease meditating on it: not, however, as a cause, in itself, of salvation, but as the sign and the "meter" of love: "God demonstrates his love towards us in the fact that, while we were still sinners, Christ died for us" (Rom 5:8).

This takes away from the Passion of Christ a connotation that has always left people perplexed and unsatisfied—that is, the idea of a price and a ransom paid to God (or, worse still, to the devil!) or of a sacrifice with which to appease divine anger. In reality, it is rather God who made the great sacrifice of giving us his Son, of not "sparing him," just as Abraham made the sacrifice of not sparing his son Isaac (Gn 22:16; Rom 8:32). God is the *subject*, no less than the *beneficiary*, of the sacrifice of the cross! It was God, in fact, who "was reconciling the world to himself in Christ, not counting their trespasses against them" (2 Cor 5:19). The Father appears to be the one who reconciles more than the one who is reconciled.

It is the New Testament itself that explains thus the Paschal Mystery of redemption. In the earliest stage of the kerygma, historical facts dominated; everything was summed up in two events: *he died—he was raised*. The phase of pure facts, however, was soon overcome. Believers asked themselves the question of the "why" of those facts—that is, of the Passion and Resurrection. The answer prompted by the Holy Spirit was that "he died *for our sins*; he was raised *for our justification*" (Rom 4:25).

There were now both the facts and the meaning of the facts for us. History and faith now formed a single Paschal Mystery; the kerygma seemed complete. But the bottom of the mystery had not yet been reached. The question was raised in another form: "And why did he die for our sins? What prompted him to do it?" The answer that brought the faith of the Church to its height was this: Because he loved us! "He loved us and for this he gave himself up for us" (Eph 5:2); "He loved me and gave himself up for me" (Gal 2:20); "He loved the Church and gave himself up for her" (Eph 5:25). It is a truth that pervades everything and applies both to the Church as a whole and to each individual person. St. John makes it the key with which to read his account of the Passion: "He loved his own in the world and he loved them to the end" (Jn 13:1).

This answer to the reason for the Passion of Christ is truly definitive and does not admit further questions. He loved us because he just loved us! St. Bernard gave a famous answer to the why—or rather, the lack of why—of love: "Love is enough for itself, pleases for himself and for his own sake. . . . Its advantage lies in its existence. I love because I love, I love to love."[2]

"I love because I love, I love to love": there is only one being, in the whole universe, who can pronounce these words with absolute truth, and that is God! For all others—including the Blessed Virgin Mary—the common law applies: "We love because he first [*protos*] loved us" (1 Jn 4:19). The love of creatures can never be "an uncaused cause," an absolute *primum*. They exist because they are loved. Even the Son of God—as we have seen—exists because he is loved by the Father. But he—and he alone—is not a creature, because he is "begotten, not made [*genitum, non factum*], of the same substance as the Father." Arriving at this distinction between being generated (*gennetòs*) and being made (*genetòs*) (just one letter of difference in Greek!) was the most arduous and decisive conquest of the Christian faith on the level of being. The year we are about to enter—2025—is the seventeenth centenary of the moment in which, at the Council of Nicaea, this light was placed on the candlestick of faith, the Credo, where it is still shining today.

2. Bernard of Clairvaux, *In Canticum*, 83, 4.

32.
A Love Worthy of God

How can we appropriate the discovered truth, transferring it from theology to life? In other words, how can we exercise the theological virtue of charity? Here is the "good news" that is never missing when we try to deepen the treasures of the Christian faith. The good news is that, thanks to our incorporation into Christ, we too can love God with a love worthy of him! Paul's affirmation that "God's love has been poured into our hearts" (Rom 5:5) cannot be fully understood except in the light of the words Jesus says to the Father: "I in them and you in me . . . that the love with which you loved me may be in them and I in them" (Jn 17:23–26).

The love that has been poured into us is the same with which the Father has always loved the Son, not a different love! It is an overflow of divine love from the Trinity to us. God communicates to the soul, writes St. John of the Cross, "the same love that he communicates to the Son, even if this does not happen by nature, as in the case of the Son, but by union. . . . The soul participates in God, carrying out, together with him, the work of the Most Holy Trinity."[1]

The consequence is that we can love the Father with the love with which the Son loves him and we can love Jesus with the love with which the Father loves him. And all this thanks to the Holy Spirit who is that very love. Scotus' requisite that God be loved in a way worthy of himself even "outside himself" (that is, outside the Trinity) has eventually been fulfilled but as a consequence, as

1. John of the Cross, *Spiritual Canticle* A, str. 38, 4.

in the second instance. And not in one person alone—that is, in the only begotten Son—but, thanks to him, in all of us.

The mystery of man's sin that causes the death of a God! The mystery of man's love that is the cause of God's joy! The true cause is always and only his love. Every slightest act of love from the soul upsets the infinite sea of God's love. It is like a pebble thrown into a lake. Is it not written that God's heart "is moved within him" and that "the innermost part of him trembles with compassion" (Hos 11:8)? It is not our love as such that has the power to "perturb" the heart of God, but his love. Because he loves us infinitely, each little "yes" of ours to his love provokes an overwhelming joy in him, for each "yes" of ours to love takes on the strength and dimension of his own love. This is because with charity we live, by grace, the love that the Father and the Son live by nature.

Our love is in itself weak, it is nothing; but by grace, it assumes the power and dimension of divine love. Thus, a father and a mother are overwhelmed with joy in their hearts when their child babbles their name or smiles for the first time. What is a baby's babbling? What is a flower that a boyfriend offers to his girlfriend? They are small acts that shock hearts and fill them with joy. This also happens in the relationship of the soul with God. The explanation is not in the cause but in the effect it provokes and in what it sets in motion.

What, then, do we give to God of our own with the theological virtue of charity, if our love is only the love we receive from him? Is there absolutely nothing new for God? Is it only a "rebound" of his own love toward him, like an echo that sends a sound back to its source, mutilated and weakened in addition? Not in this case, God be praised! The echo returns to God from the cavern of our hearts but with a novelty that is everything for God: the scent of our freedom and our filial gratitude! All this is accomplished, in an exemplary way, in the Eucharist. In it we present to the Father as "our offering" what the Father has first given us—that is, his Son, Jesus. Our love for God can only be a return wave.

We can say to God the Father: "Father, I love you with the love with which your Son Jesus loves you"; and we can say to Jesus: "Jesus, I love you with the love with which your heavenly Father loves you," and know with certainty (it is theological faith!) that all this is not a pious figment of the imagination! St. Paul has written, "Put on the Lord Jesus Christ" (Rom 13:14), and again, "Your life is hidden with Christ in God" (Col 3:3). Disguised as Christ, we stealthily enter, even now, before God and dwell in the Trinity!

Every time I try, in prayer, to do this myself, I am reminded of the episode of Jacob who presents himself to his father Isaac to receive the blessing, pretending to be his elder brother (Gn 27:1–23). And I try to imagine what God the Father might say to himself at that moment: "The voice is not really that of my firstborn Son; but the hands, the feet, and the whole body are the same that my Son took on down there on earth and brought up here to heaven."

And I am sure he blesses me, just as Isaac blessed Jacob!

33.
If God Loved Us So Much . . .

It is time to come down from the heights of the Trinity to the earth of our daily life. Thus far, we are only halfway in our exploration of the vast continent of charity. God's love is without conditions but not without consequences! Our discourse on love would remain an unfinished sentence, like a protasis not followed by an apodosis. The protasis is "If God loved us so much"; the apodosis is "we too must love each other." Here, we see how the *gift* is the foundation of the *commandment* and how the two are wonderfully at peace with each other in Christianity, in vital and intrinsic continuity. There is not *gift* on the one hand and *duty* on the other; *grace* on the one hand, *law* on the other. Rather, there is the gift that creates duty, the grace that enhances the law, taking it up into its service. The liberal theology of the nineteenth century had reduced "the essence of Christianity" to little more than a vague "let us love each other!" It focused on the apodosis, completely skipping the protasis "If God loved us so much," with all this sentence entails: the Trinity and the Death and Resurrection of Christ. We should avoid committing the opposite error.

What is the commandment deriving from God's love for us? We immediately think—and rightly so—of the "first and greatest of the commandments," that of loving the Lord God with all our heart, with all our soul, and with all our strength. It is God himself who not only allows us but even asks us to love him, making this the "first commandment."

Love is the only field in which the creature can rival God and, as it were, repay him with the same coin. If God is angry with me, can I be angry with him? If he scolds me, can I start scolding him? If he judges me, can I start judging him too? Certainly not! This, on the contrary, is lawful in love. He loves me and I can love him back, and the more he loves me, the more I can love him.[1]

Let us remember, however, what we have said above: to love God is the first commandment in the order of intention, not of execution. It is the greatest, but it does not come first. First (that is, in order of time or execution), something else comes—the second commandment, which, for this reason, is called "similar to the first": "You shall love your neighbor as yourself."

The great law of natural love is reciprocity: as I have loved you, so you love me; the great law of theological love, on the other hand, is circularity. "Beloved, if God so loved us . . ." At this point we would expect the sentence to end with the words "we too must love him." But no: ". . . we also must love one another" (1 Jn 4:11). It is a constant rule: "He laid down his life for us; so we ought to lay down our lives for our brothers" (1 Jn 3:16). "Love one another as I love you" (Jn 15:12). After Easter, Jesus asks Peter, "Do you love me?" Peter replies: "I love you, Lord!" and Jesus: "Feed my sheep!" (Jn 21:15–17). "I will lay down my life for you," says Peter. "Do you want to give your life for me?"— Jesus seems to mean—"Then give it for my sheep!"

The Trinitarian process—from the Father, to the Son, in the Holy Spirit—is reflected in history. The love of the Father becomes visible in the Son; from the Son, through the work of the Holy Spirit, it comes to us; from us—always through the work of the Holy Spirit—it must rebound to our neighbor: "As the Father

---

1. Bernard of Clairvaux, *In Canticum*, 83, 4.

loves me, so I also love you. . . . Love one another as I love you" (Jn 15:9, 12).

Why this singular diversion of love from God to neighbor? The most immediate reason is this. We still live in the flesh; everything has to go through the flesh. Love, too, must be incarnate to be authentic and not disembodied, thus fading into nothingness. Therefore, not being possible to love God in this concrete and practical way, with soul and with hands, because God cannot be seen, we are directed to the neighbor who can be seen: in fact, "Whoever does not love their neighbor, whom they see, cannot love God, whom they do not see" (1 Jn 4:20). The neighbor, the other, is the visible face of God for me. St. Catherine of Siena adds another equally fundamental motivation. She has God saying:

> I ask you to love me with the same love with which I love you. But for me you cannot do this, for I loved you without being loved. Whatever love you have for me you owe me, so you love me not gratuitously but out of duty, while I love you not out of duty but gratuitously. So you cannot give me the kind of love I ask of you. This is why I have put you among your neighbors: so that you can do for them what you cannot do for me—that is, love them without any concern for thanks and without looking for any profit for yourself. And whatever you do for them I will consider done for me.[2]

In the meantime, what about the commandment to love God—that is, him in person—"with all your heart and with all your soul"? Is it suspended, or identified purely and simply with the commandment to love one's neighbor? This has sometimes been the solution of the so-called "Theology of Secularization," making Christianity "the religion of the second commandment."

2. Catherina of Siena, *Dialogue*, 64.

But nothing of this! The commandment to love God remains always valid; it is the very reason why we love our neighbor, and it is exercised in every act of loving others. There is an absolute reciprocity between the two. They are like two connected doors that open and close together. It is written that one loves God if one loves one's neighbor; but it is also written that we love our neighbor if we love God: "In this way we know that we love the children of God when we love God" (1 Jn 5:2).

Of course, this indirect way of loving God and Christ, as through a third party, is not the only one possible. There is a direct way, from person to person, which is our greatest happiness in life and it consists in being loved by God and in loving him with both *agape* and *eros*. This will be the subject of the following chapter.

34.
Eros and *Agape*: Love and Charity

What relationship is there between the theological virtue of charity and the love understood in the most common and daily sense of the term—that is, love between friends, between engaged couples, between spouses, of parents for children, of children for parents? A convincing answer must be given to this question lest we relegate the theological virtue of charity to a kind of spiritual *hyperuranion* detached from all human experience.

There is a work that has spread throughout the intellectual Christian world the thesis of the incompatibility of the two forms of love.[1] *Eros* and *agape* designate, according to this vision, two opposite movements: the first, *eros*, indicates man's ascent to God as to his own good and to his own origin; the second, *agape*, indicates God's descent toward humanity in the Incarnation and on the cross. *Agape*, in other words, is the salvation offered to man without merit and without any response from him other than faith alone. St. Paul would be the one who most purely understood and formulated this doctrine of love. After him, this radical antithesis was allegedly lost, to give rise to attempts at a synthesis between the love of God and love for God. The thesis of "sola fides" with the exclusion of works leads to the formula of "sola caritas" (*agape*) with the exclusion of *eros*.

---

1. Anders Nygren, *Agape and Eros*, Westminster Press, Harper & Row, 1936 (Original: *Eros och Agape*, Stockholm, 1930–1936).

The backlash of this operation is the radical worldliness and secularization of *eros*. While, in fact, a certain theology excluded *eros* from *agape*, secular culture, for its part, was more than happy to do the opposite, removing *agape* from *eros*—that is, eliminating from human love any reference to God and grace. Freud went all the way along this line, reducing love to *eros* and *eros* to libido. It is the stage to which love is reduced in many manifestations of life and culture, especially in the entertainment world: that of sexual attraction, sex appeal and nothing more.

Unintentionally, the thesis of the irreconcilability of the two loves gives a theological justification to what, in fact, had always been thought about the relationship between *eros* and *agape*. Western art, from the Renaissance onward, is full of representations of the two loves at war with each other. The title "Sacred love and profane love" given (not by the author!) to a famous painting by Titian is significant, while, in reality, it does not represent two opposing loves but two faces of the same love, indeed the conjugal love.[2]

If we cannot change the idea of love that the world has, we can, however, correct the theological vision which—certainly unwittingly—favors and legitimizes it. This is what Benedict XVI did with the encyclical "Deus caritas est." He reaffirms the traditional Catholic synthesis by expressing it in modern terms: "*Eros* and *agape*—ascending love and descending love—can never be completely separated. . . . Biblical faith does not set up a parallel universe, or one opposed to that primordial human phenomenon which is love, but rather accepts the whole man; it intervenes in his search for love in order to purify it and to reveal new dimensions of it" (no. 7–8).

2. The painting, kept in the Galleria Borghese in Rome, according to today's interpretation, celebrates a wedding, and it is unthinkable that the painter wanted to remind the couple that theirs was a "profane love" and that there was another different love that was nobler than theirs! The two women in the picture—very similar to each other; one half-naked, the other dressed with symbols of fertility and domestic life around her—actually indicate the same person: first bride, then mother!

Eros and *agape* are united in the very source of love which is God: "God loves, and his love may certainly be called *eros*, yet it is also totally *agape*" (no. 9). In other words, God's love for us is itself both erotic and agapeic. God, in the Bible, does not love us out of pity and mercy; he desires us, he wants to be loved in return, he compares himself to a jealous lover and husband. "When God loves, he wants nothing more than to be loved. He loves not for anything else, if not to be loved, knowing that those who will love him will enjoy this same love. . . . The love of the Spouse, or rather the nuptial-love, seeks only love and fidelity in return."[3]

In us, unlike in God, the two components of love—*eros* and *agape*, love of desire and love of giving—are not in peace and harmony with each other. In the beginning, the love of concupiscence predominates, taking rather than giving. This is why Pope Benedicts XVI speaks of the need for a progressive "purification" of *eros* toward "new dimensions" of love, both in married life and in any other form of love.

Those who support the thesis of the incompatibility between *eros* and *agape* stress the fact that the New Testament carefully avoids—and, apparently, deliberately—the term *eros*, always and only using *agape* in its place (apart from the rare use of *philia*, which indicates the love of friendship). The Latin translators of the Bible have tried to keep this choice, translating *agape* with *caritas* (from *carus*, dear) rather than with *amor*.

The philological datum, therefore, is true, but the conclusions drawn from it are not true. It is assumed that the authors of the New Testament have in mind both the meaning that the term *eros* had in the common language—the so-called "vulgar *eros*"—and the elevated and philosophical meaning it had, for example, in Plato: the so-called "noble *eros*." In the popular sense, *eros* indicated more or less what it means today when we talk about eroticism or erotic films—that is, the satisfaction of the sexual

3. Bernard of Clairvaux, *In Canticum*, 83, 4–5.

instinct. In the noble meaning, *eros* meant the love of beauty, the strength that holds the world together and pushes all beings to unity. In other words, the movement of ascent toward the divine that some dialectical theologians consider incompatible with the movement of the divine descent toward humanity.

It is difficult to argue that the authors of the New Testament, initially addressing simple people, intended to warn them of Plato's *eros*. They avoided the term *eros* for the same reason that a preacher today avoids the term erotic or, if he uses it, does it only in the negative sense. The reason is that, both then as now, the word *eros* usually stands for love in its most selfish and sensual expression.[4]

However, as soon as Christianity comes into cultural contact with the Greek world and with the Platonic vision—already with Origen in the third century—there is a revaluation of *eros* as an upward movement of the soul toward good and as a universal attraction exercised by beauty and the divine. *Eros* is often used in Greek authors as a synonym for *agape* and can indicate God's love for man and man's love for God as well as love for virtues and for everything beautiful. In a very special way, *eros* indicates the type of love that must be nurtured for Christ, the God-man: "Human love [*eros*] is foreordained to him, as his model and end."[5]

The same evolution is noted in the Latin world. *Caritas* tends more and more to designate charity toward one's neighbor, while with *amor*, the highest forms of love are expressed, up to the mystical love for God and for Christ. In the commentaries on the *Song of Songs*, the word "love" is much more frequent than "charity."

The rehabilitation of *eros* not only helps consecrated persons to make their love pass from the will to the heart, it also helps, first of all, human lovers and Christian spouses, showing them the

4. Pseudo-Dionysius the Areopagite, *De divinis nominibus*, IV, 12 (PG 3, 709), already explains in this way the reason why the authors of the New Testament avoid the term *eros*.

5. Nicolas Cabasilas, *Vita in Christo*, II, 9 (PG 150, 560).

beauty and dignity of the love that unites them. It helps young people to experience the fascination of sex not as something murky, to be lived away from God, but on the contrary as a gift from the Creator for their joy, if lived in the order he wanted— that is, united to, or at least tending toward, *agape*. All true love is "sacred." Something of its sacredness remains even in its most squalid deformations, because "love is from God" (1 Jn 4:7).

35.
Love and Do
What You Want!

Unfortunately, the word "charity" is no longer able to express the whole content of the theological virtue that carries its name. The reason is that with the passing of time it has ended up being identified with "works of charity." The phrase "doing charity" is revealing: charity is more something you "do" rather than something you "have"! All religious orders and congregations that have the word "charity" in their name are realities that operate in the field of corporal or spiritual works of mercy. "Caritas," in addition, is the name of an international organization that works for the poor.

If we want to continue to call the third theological virtue by this name, we need to rediscover the primordial meaning of the word *agape*, translated as charity. We must start with St. Paul, the "theorist" of *agape* in the New Testament. He begins his long parenesis on love with an affirmation that contains the essence of it in a nutshell: "Let love [*agape*] be sincere!" (Rom 12:9). The original term used by St. Paul that is translated "sincere" is *anhypòkritos*—that is, without hypocrisy. It is a term that we find used almost exclusively in the New Testament to define Christian love. It also occurs in 2 Corinthians (6:6) and in the First Letter of Peter (1:22). This last text allows us to grasp with all certainty the meaning of the term because it explains it with a periphrasis;

sincere love—it says—consists in loving each other intensely "from the heart."

St. Paul takes the discourse to the very root of charity, to the heart. What is required of love is that it be true, authentic, and not fake. This is a faithful echo of the teaching of Jesus, who had pointed to the heart as the place where the moral value of what a person does is decided (Mt 15:19). The phrase "Charity must not be hypocritical" seems almost the translation of the saying of Jesus: "When you give alms, do not blow a trumpet before you, as the hypocrites do" (Mt 6:2).

We can speak of a Pauline insight regarding charity. It consists in revealing, behind the visible and external universe of charity made up of works and words, another entirely interior universe, which, in relation to the first, is what the soul is for the body. We find this insight in the other great text on charity, which is 1 Corinthians 13. What St. Paul says there all refers to this interior charity, to the dispositions and sentiments of charity: charity is patient, it is benign, it is not envious, it is not angry, it covers everything, believes everything, hopes everything. Nothing is said concerning the external act of doing good or works of charity, but rather everything is brought back to the root of love. *Beneficence* must come from *benevolence*.

It is the Apostle himself who highlights the difference between the two spheres of charity. He says that the greatest act of external charity (distributing all one's substance to the poor) would be useless without interior charity; it would be the opposite of "sincere" charity. Hypocritical charity, in fact, is precisely that which does something good without loving and shows outside what has no equivalent in the heart. In this case, there is a façade of charity, which can, at the limit, hide self-seeking, exploitation of the brother, or even sheer remorse of conscience.

It would be a fatal mistake to contrast charity of the heart and charity of the facts or take refuge in the interior charity to find an alibi in it for the lack of effective charity. We know how vigorously the words of Jesus (Mt 25), of St. James (2:16), and of St. John (1 Jn 3:18) push toward the charity of facts. We know the importance that St. Paul himself gave to collections for the poor of Jerusalem. Moreover, to say that, without charity, even giving everything to the poor benefits me "to nothing" does not mean that this is of no use to anyone; it rather means that it does not benefit me, while it can benefit the poor who receive it. It is therefore not a question of attenuating the importance of works of charity, but rather of ensuring in them a secure foundation against selfishness and its infinite tricks. St. Paul wants Christians to be "rooted and grounded in charity" (Eph 3:17), that charity be the root and foundation of everything.

God himself established this foundation when he said: "You shall love your neighbor as yourself!" (Mt 22:39). He could not assure love of neighbor on a better "peg" than this one; he would not have achieved the same goal even if he had said "You shall love your neighbor as your God!" About the love of God—that is, what it is to love God—man can still cheat, but about the love of himself, no. In every circumstance, people know very well what they would want others to do or to say to them; this is a mirror that they always have in front of them. Taking up Paul's teaching, St. Augustine said, "Love and do what you want":

> This brief precept is imposed on you once and for all: love and do what you want. If you are silent, be silent for love; if you speak, speak for love; if you correct, correct for love; if you forgive, forgive for love. Put the root of love in your heart, since from this root nothing but good can proceed.[1]

At times, this rule of St. Augustine has been looked upon with suspicion. Is this not precisely the reason some give to justify

---

1. Augustine, *On the First Letter of John*, 7, 8: "Ama et fac quod vis."

any sort of disorder in the field of love? But St. Augustine speaks of true love, not of selfishness in disguise.

The capacity and natural predisposition of the human being to love and be loved is the only thing that can save our technological civilization from a progressive dehumanization. Years ago, I took part in a public debate in London. The moderator posed a series of questions on ecology and modern technology to a panel that consisted of a theology professor from Yale University, an Anglican bishop, and myself. The crucial point was this: after replacing man's operational abilities with robots, technique is now on the verge of replacing his mental abilities with artificial intelligence. What then remains that is exclusive to a human being? Are we still indispensable to nature?

When it was my turn to answer, I made a simple reflection. We are working, I said, on a computer that thinks, but can we imagine a computer that loves, that is moved by our pains and rejoices in our joys? We can conceive of artificial intelligence, but can we conceive of an artificial love? Is it not, then, precisely here that we must place the specific quality of the human being and the inalienable attribute of it? For a believer there is a reason that explains this fact, and it is that we were created in the image of God. And "God is love"!

If we ask ourselves why we are so eager to know and so little concerned about loving, the answer is simple: knowledge translates into power, love into service!

At the end of his philosophical reflections on the danger of technology for modern society, Martin Heidegger, almost throwing in the towel, exclaimed: "Only a god can save us!"[2] We can paraphrase: "Only love can save us!"

---

2. Martin Heidegger, *Antwort: Martin Heidegger im Gespräch*, Gesamtausgabe, vol. 16, Frankfurt, 1975.

36.
Charity, a Social Virtue

Charity "edifies." Scripture attributes this prerogative almost exclusively to it: "Knowledge inflates with pride, but love builds up" (1 Cor 8:1). What does it build up? First of all, the edifice of God, which is the Church!

> Living the truth in love, we should grow in every way into him who is the head, Christ from whom the whole body, joined and held together by every supporting ligament, with the proper functioning of each part, brings about the body's growth and builds itself up in love. (Eph 4:15–16)

The Church is built with charity; its level of growth is determined by the level of growth in charity. Charity is the "society of saints"—that is, what constitutes the invisible reality of the Church. It is the reality (*res*) of the sacrament, the meaning of the sign that is the visible Church. "Charity endures" (1 Cor 13:13). It is the only one that remains. Once the Scriptures, faith, hope, charisms, ministries, and everything else cease, charity remains. Everything will disappear as when the scaffolding used to build an edifice is dismantled and what was previously hidden appears in its full splendor.

Charity, like hope, is not resolved in the personal sphere but is an eminently social virtue. In the work *The City of God*, which informed Christian thought throughout the Middle Ages, St. Augustine explains that two cities coexist in history: the city of Satan

155

(today we would say "the city of the sinful man"!) symbolized by Babylon, and the city of God symbolized by Jerusalem. What distinguishes the two companies is the different love by which they are moved. The first has as its motive the "love of self pushed to the point of contempt of God"; the second has as its motive the "love of God pushed to the point of contempt of self."[1]

The opposition, in this case, is between love of God and love of oneself. In another work, St. Augustine partially corrects this opposition, or at least balances it.[2] The real contrast that characterizes the two cities is not between the love of God and the love of oneself (these two loves, correctly understood, can—indeed must—exist together). No, the real contrast is internal to self-love, and it is the opposition between the exclusive love of self, *amor privatus*, and the love of the common good, *amor socialis*. It is the echo of the Pauline exhortation not to seek only one's own interest but also that of others (Phil 2:4). It is private love—that is, selfishness—that creates the city of Satan, Babylon, and it is social love that creates the city of God, where harmony and peace reign.

Social love is just another name for the second commandment: "You shall love your neighbor as yourself." Jesus did not limit himself to relaunching this commandment already present in the Hebrew Testament, but he gave it a new foundation. He said: "This is my commandment: love one another as I love you" (Jn 15:12). No longer as we love ourselves but as Christ loved us. And we know how he loved us! The greatest novelty is not even the example of love he has left us. Jesus did something new and unheard of: he identified himself with our neighbor, especially with those whom he calls "the least of my brothers" (Mt 25:40): the hungry, the thirsty, the naked, the sick, the strangers, and the prisoners. The first and second commandments have become like

1. Augustine, *De civitate Dei*, 14, 28: "amor sui usque ad contemptum Dei"—"amor Dei usque ad contemptum sui."

2. Augustine, *De Genesi ad litteram*, 11, 15, 20 (PL 32, 582).

communicating vessels, almost a single commandment. "You did it to me" and "You did not do it to me"! Christian salvation can never be an exclusively personal matter that is decided between oneself and God.

Some great theoreticians of economic sciences have affirmed—and everyday reality proves them right—that the spring of human action, and in particular of economy, is personal interest and profit. This is stronger than any ideology based on the common good, on the love of one's country, or on the construction of the society of tomorrow. (Those who want to buy a car do not consider whether it is of national or foreign production, but whether or not it meets their personal needs!)

The Gospel of Christ is perfectly in agreement with this—that is, about the priority of the personal over any other motivation of human action. However, it reveals, at the same time, what is the true and supreme personal interest of the human person and how, correctly understood, it is not the enemy of the common good but its most powerful ally. Jesus said: "What profit is there for one to gain the whole world yet lose or forfeit himself?" (Lk 9:25). What "personal interest" can there be more decisive than to save one's life for eternity?

37.
Faith, Hope, and Charity:
A Christian Antidote
to Nihilism

In the introduction, I mentioned the challenges that the three theological virtues must face in the modern world. One of them—perhaps the most radical—is that of nihilism. I speak of the nihilism that places the Nothing (here a metaphysical category) in the place of God. It found its perfect expression in the well-known proclamation that Friedrich Nietzsche puts in the mouth of the "madman" arriving breathless to the town square:

> Where has God gone?—he shouted—I want to tell you! It was we who killed him: you and me! . . . There was never a greater action: all those who come after us will belong, by virtue of this action, to a higher story than all the stories told to date.[1]

In the logic of these words (and, I believe, in the author's expectations), history after him would no longer be divided into "before Christ" and "after Christ" but into "before Nietzsche" and "after Nietzsche."

Apparently, it is not the Nothing that is put in the place of God but man, and more precisely, the "super-man"; but it will not be long in realizing that, left alone, man is himself nothing:

1. Friedrich Nietzsche, *The Gay Science*, n. 125.

What did we ever do to loosen this earth from the chain of its sun? Where is it moving now? Where are we moving to? Away from all the suns? Isn't ours an eternal falling? And backwards, to the side, forward, and on all sides? Is there still an up and a down? Are we not wandering as through an infinite nothing?

The reassuring implicit answer of the "madman" to these disturbing questions of his is "No, because man will carry out the task up to now assigned to God." Instead, our answer is "Yes, and that is exactly what happened and is happening: 'Wandering as through an infinite nothing!'"

The believer today has to face a more radical error than the one Paul, Augustine, and Luther had to fight in their time: not the error of wanting to save oneself by one's own strength but that of not wanting to be saved at all! To be, if anything, saviors not saved. People no longer think, with Ivan Karamazov, of returning their ticket to God: they simply tear it up! It is not just a question of the belief that God doesn't exist—that is, of sheer atheism. It is the will—or rather the pretension—that he must not exist. The Greeks coined a term to express (and to condemn) this kind of arrogance toward the divinity, the term *hubris*.

It is not up to us to judge the heart of a man that only God knows. Nietzsche, too, had his fair share of suffering in life, and suffering unites with Christ perhaps more than invectives separate from him. Jesus' prayer on the cross "Father, forgive them, for they do not know what they are doing" (Lk 23:34) was not only pronounced in favor of those present! An image comes to my mind that I have sometimes observed in person and that I hope has become reality in the meantime. An angry child tries to hit his father's face with punches and scratches, until, exhausted, he falls crying into his father's arms, who soothes him and presses him to his chest.

This does not exclude the possibility that God may have used

Nietzsche (as he used others of his class in other fields) to remind Christians of some unpleasant but true facts: for example, that they used to speak more often about death than about life, more about grief than about joy. For that we must be grateful to him, without forgetting that our true Master told us these things well before Nietzsche did. Another, not insubstantial, "merit" must be acknowledged in Nietzsche: that of not choosing an easy target for his critique—that is, "Religion"—as many of his predecessors and contemporaries (Hegel, Feuerbach, Marx, Freud) had done, but of having clearly seen the true "front" where the decisive battle takes place, the person and teaching of Jesus Christ.

God guards us, therefore, from the sin of arrogating to ourselves the right to judge the final outcome of a titanic and exceptionally gifted spirit. The Christian's sentiment toward Nietzsche should be inspired by that, full of respect for the mystery, which Alessandro Manzoni expressed at the death of Napoleon:

> Let us in reverence bow
> Before the One who chose
> Of his creator spirit
> In him a larger trace to print.[2]

Manzoni, however, asks himself the question: "Fu vera gloria?" Was it true glory? And rightly so, because it is not the skill in fighting that makes the hero but the cause for which he fights.

Let us not judge, I repeat, the person whom only God knows. The consequence that Nietzsche's proclamation has had, however, is something we can and must judge. It has been used in the most diverse ways, to the point of becoming a fashion, an atmosphere that reigns in the intellectual circles of the "postmodern" Western world.[3] At the time of Romanticism, people used to bask in

2. Alessandro Manzoni, *Cinque Maggio* (*The Fifth of May*; my own translation).
3. The Extropian program of transhumanism of the late '80s was but an update of Nietzsche's super-humanism.

melancholy; today, they bask in nihilism. Few names have been cited more often and with more religious devotion than that of Nietzsche in the century that we have behind us. How many who, perhaps, consider themselves believers in Christ continue to "flirt" with someone who has declared in every possible way that he wanted to be his direct antagonist.

My aim is to show, from a deeper point of view than the philosophical one (for there is, with all due respect to Hegel, a point of view superior to that of philosophy!), what lies behind that proclamation: the sinister flicker of an ancient flame, the sudden eruption of a volcano that has never been extinguished since the beginning of the world.

The story, according to biblical revelation, began even before the appearance of humankind on earth. The human drama, too, had its "prologue in heaven," in that "spirit of negation" that could not accept that its existence was thanks to another. He is the "morning star" personified, according to Isaiah, by the king of Babylon who said in his heart: "I will make myself equal to the Most High" (Is 14:13). Since then, he has been recruiting supporters for his cause. The first—to whom he showed himself under the guise of a serpent—were, according to the Bible, the naïve Adam and Eve.

All this seems to modern man nothing more than an etiological myth to explain the existence of evil in the world. And in the positive sense given to myth today, such it is! But history, literature (Goethe's *Faust!*), and our own personal experience tell us that behind this "myth" there is a transcendent truth that no historical or philosophical reasoning could convey to us.

> To be, or not to be, that is the question:
> . . . To die—to sleep,
> No more; and by a sleep to say we end.[4]

4. William Shakespeare, *Hamlet*, act III, sc. 1.

Shakespeare has nothing to do with Nietzsche. The context is different here: not that of a challenge, but rather of tiredness in fighting. Read today, however, these famous words of Hamlet, at least to me, sound like this: "Why being, rather than nothing? Why are we not spared the trouble of existing and allowed to rest in an eternal sleep, unaware of everything?" And we could continue with Job: "Why did I not die at birth? . . . / For then I should have lain down and been tranquil; / had I slept, I should then have been at rest" (Job 3:11–13).

With those words put in the mouth of Hamlet (often quoted lightly and almost as a joke), Shakespeare makes the tragic aspect of human life flash before our eyes. One night, as if from afar and as a warning, I glimpsed the true face of this temptation—that is, rejecting existence, seeing it as a being "thrown into it," without our knowledge and despite ourselves. I shivered and began to pray, remembering Jesus in the desert. If human beings knew while alive, as they will at the moment of death, what it means to reject God and one's own existence, they would die of terror. Not wanting to exist thanks to another, and yet not being able to annihilate oneself and escape that superior power, is the formula of pure desperation. It doesn't consist in the eternal *death* they desire, but in an eternal *dying*.[5] Perhaps this is the worm that does not die and the fire that is not quenched of which Jesus speaks in the Gospel (Mk 9:48).

I know it well: what Nietzsche intended to substitute for faith in God is not a passive resignation and the will to die, but rather the opposite. "The purpose I set for myself," he wrote to a female friend, "requires a heroic way of thinking and certainly not a religious resignation."[6] He has written:

---

5. Kierkegaard, *The Sickness unto Death*, Part I, C.
6. Friedrich Nietzsche, Letter to Malwida von Meysenbug, in Manuscripts, III, 2, p. 222.

> The weak and the botched shall perish: first principle of *our* charity. And one should help them to it.
>
> What is more harmful than any vice?—Practical sympathy for the botched and the weak—Christianity.[7]

Of the new man resulting from this "inversion of all values," we are entitled to exclaim—with a sense of satisfaction and pride, no longer of compassion—"*Ecce homo!*" Here is the man![8] At the end of all his *negations*—of God, of the past, of the present, of the future ("an eternal return" of the past!), of philosophers, of priests, and of everything—only one *affirmation* remains: that of himself. Perhaps God used this man to make us see, as if by amplification, what is there, more or less latent, in the depths of each of us, without his grace. The story of Nietzsche—much more rightly than that of Abraham—should be read "with fear and trembling."

Modern nihilism cannot be overcome by inventing a new philosophical theory or by modulating the radical one of its progenitor. Many have tried, in good faith, to do it after him: "The true thought of him was not understood; his concept of superman has been misunderstood" and so on. Someone even tried to make him an apologist for the "true Christianity" intended by Jesus, against that of the Church and traditional Western culture. I wonder if Nietzsche would be happy being tamed in this way.

God knows how proud we are and has come to help us. He has shown us that he is not "that Oriental greedy for honors in his heavenly home."[9] He "annihilated himself" before our eyes, presenting himself, in Christ, reduced to nothing, deprived of power, dignity, prestige, and life. "God? We killed him: you and me!":

7. *The Antichrist*, 2, trans. H.L. Mencken. It is chilling to read these words after Hitler so literally implemented them, half a century later. Some modern commentators do not seem to be troubled by them, and they say that those who are troubled "have understood nothing about Nietzsche."

8. Friedrich Nietzsche, *Ecce homo*, 1888 (published in 1908).

9. Friedrich Nietzsche, *The Gay Science*, n. 135.

this terrible thing did, in fact, happen once in human history but in a quite different sense from that shouted by the "madman." The Resurrection of Christ from the dead assures us, however, that this path does not lead to defeat but to that "apotheosis of life" in vain sought elsewhere.

These reflections of mine, like all the rest of this book, do not have a polemic or apologetic intention but a pastoral one. The aim is to keep believers—and who knows, maybe just a few young university students—from being drawn into this vortex of nihilism, which is the true "black hole" of the spiritual universe. It is not just "the sleep of reason" that "produces monsters" but also its delirium. How topical is Dante's warning:

> Christians, be ye more serious in your movements;
> Be ye not like a feather at each wind,
> And think not every water washes you.[10]

Our positive aim is to rediscover the beauty of the three theological virtues. Faith, hope, and charity are like "three life jackets" to be thrown to those who struggle among the stormy waves of life.

---

10. *Paradise*, V, 73–75 (trans. Longfellow).

38.
Praying with the Three Theological Virtues

The three theological virtues—as we have repeatedly empha-sized—are each present in the other. They are "perichoretic," like the three persons of the Trinity! Let us try to capture the moment when, more clearly than ever, they act in accord. This special mo-ment is prayer. In it, faith, hope, and charity are "caught in the act" (in theology, we say, "*in actu exercito*")—that is, in the very exercise of their function. Indeed, the essence of prayer is "the desire for God that springs from faith, hope and charity."[1]

For centuries, Christian piety has handed down from par-ents to children three short prayers that are, respectively, the acts of faith, hope, and charity. With small variations, they sound like this:

> *Act of faith*: My God, I believe everything you have revealed and the holy Church proposes us to believe, because you are infallible truth. And I expressly believe in you, the only true God in three equal and distinct persons: Father, Son, and Holy Spirit. And I believe in Jesus Christ, the Son of God incarnate, who died and rose for us, who will give each one, according their merit, the reward or eternal punishment.

> *Act of hope*: My God, I hope from your goodness, for your

1. Augustine, *Letters*, 130, 9.

165

promises and for the merits of Jesus Christ our Savior, eternal life and the graces necessary to merit it with the good works that I must and want to do. Lord, may I enjoy you forever.

Act of charity: My God, I love you with all my heart above all things, because you are infinite good and our eternal happiness; and for your love I love my neighbor as myself and I forgive the offenses received. Lord, may I love you more and more.

The most appropriate time to recite these acts is in the morning, upon awakening. Faith, hope, and charity are like those good old housewives who, in the morning, got up first and woke up the rest of the family. To tell the truth, they themselves need to be awakened, and this is what the Holy Spirit does. Night is a relapse into the unconscious; dreams are a vestige of primordial chaos. Every morning, upon awakening, we need the Holy Spirit hovering again over the darkness and chaos, as at the beginning of the world, to transform it into the light and harmony of a new creation.

Traditional acts of faith, hope, and charity remain a model; but it is not forbidden to exchange them with others similar in content, perhaps more spontaneous and suited to the state and situation one lives in. Among other things, these traditional acts have a limit we have often pointed to. They highlight almost exclusively the objective aspect of the theological virtues—what to believe, what to hope for, what to love—not the subjective and existential aspect of them. The act of charity especially has a serious limit. "My God, I love you with all my heart": in such sentence God is, again and always, a God to be loved, more than a God who loves. By now, we know that more important than our love for God is God's love for us. The act of charity should not always begin by saying "My God, I love you with all my heart" but sometimes by saying "My God, I believe with all my heart that you love me."

Now let us broaden our horizons on the vast panorama of Christian prayer. Let us consider two praying people, placed at opposite ends of the spectrum: a beginner and a perfect one. And let us take them in one of the two different situations described by Jesus in the Gospel: not in the Temple, like the Pharisee and the tax collector, but after people entered their room and closed the door behind them (Mt 6:6)—that is to say, in personal prayer.

What does it imply when a man or a woman—better if both together as husband and wife—before going to bed in the evening make the sign of the cross and recite a short prayer, give thanks for the day if it was good, offer it if it was heavy, and ask protection for their children and loved ones? Well, they have made the fundamental act of faith! No matter how much routine and habit there may be in their prayer, it shows that they believe that there is a God and that each of them is under the gaze of this God. No one would speak to a wall! They also tacitly made an act of hope and charity. They proclaimed with facts that the God they turned to is a loving God who listens and cares about them and their small (or big) problems. Nobody confides their pains and feelings to someone supposed to be indifferent, and nobody would pray if they did not hope to be granted what they are asking for.

Let us now shift our focus to the other praying person, the perfect one. In order not to remain vague, let us also give her a name: Anjezë Gonxhe Bojaxhiu, or, as everyone calls her, Mother Teresa of Kolkata. In addition to being the woman of charity, the whole world knew her as the woman who always prayed: all the time with the rosary in her hands (even at the moment of receiving the Nobel Peace Prize) or motionless in adoration before the Blessed Sacrament. After her death, her intimate diaries and reports to her spiritual father were made public. She had tried in every possible way to make them disappear, but a copy had survived, thanks to her bishop, who had "disobeyed" her. In them, Mother Teresa said she no longer had faith, hope, or charity. Reading this, some shouted at the scandal: "Then it was all a show!" Some even spoke of a secret atheism of Mother Teresa. In one of her writings to her confessor, she said:

> In my soul I feel just that terrible pain of loss—of God not wanting me—of God not being God—of God not really existing. . . . Heaven, what emptiness—not a single thought of Heaven enters my mind—for there is no hope. . . . In my heart there is no faith, no love, no trust.[2]

Mother Teresa is not the first or the only one to speak like this. Another mystic, St. Catherine of Genoa, centuries earlier, had written about herself: "Faith is lost, hope is dead."[3] How can this be explained? Was their life really a deception? The truth is quite the opposite. These souls had reached, or were in the process of reaching, perfect faith, hope, and charity. A faith that believes "without having seen," a hope that hopes "against all hope," a love that loves without being (read, feeling!) loved. Mother Teresa, who wrote the words just quoted, in one of her prayers, says to Jesus:

> If my separation from you brings others to you—why Jesus, I am willing with all my heart to suffer all that I suffer, not only now, but for eternity, if this was possible. Your happiness is all that I want.[4]

Mother Teresa lived the last fifty years of her life in terrible interior darkness, hiding her pain in heroic silence and always giving others her smile and tireless support. The desire that every memory of her inner state disappear was not dictated by the fear

---

2. Mother Teresa: *Come Be My Light: The Private Writings of the "Saint of Calcutta,"* Doubleday Religion, 2007, pp. 192–193.

3. Catherine of Genoa, *Life*, chap. 19.

4. *Come Be My Light*, cit., p. 194.

of leaving a bad image of herself but, on the contrary, by the desire not to be taken for a saint and a mystic, knowing well, in the depth of her heart, that those trials were the sign of a very high and demanding journey with God, which she shared with a host of other chosen souls.

How far from the truth are those theological currents that reject the very idea of a Christian mysticism and that oppose, as a higher value, pure faith to the *experience* of the divine! The interior life of true Christian mystics, seen from their own writings (and not just from the writings about them!), is the strongest demonstration of the annihilation of the human reliance on one's own virtues and of the claims to be saved by one's own merits. It is the experience that most radiates the absolute sovereignty of God's action and grace.

Equally far from the truth is the vast group of psychologists, historians, and commentators of art who, in front of Bernini's *Ecstasy of Saint Teresa* and other similar pieces of art, immediately speak, with great assurance, of a disguised or sublimated sensual love. It is no wonder that the artists deliberately favored this interpretation (they were artists, not mystics!); nor is it surprising that this interpretation corresponds, unfortunately, to the truth in so many pseudo-mystics. However, it is completely false when it comes to true mystics. Sexual love has no place in them except as a symbol. Mystics have lived what Goethe says at the end of his *Faust*: "All of the transient / Is parable, only."[5]

There is a reason why God's love, starting from the Bible, is usually expressed with the symbol of nuptial love. It is because spousal love is the only truly free love among all the various forms of love. The fact that you are your sister's brother or even that you are the father of your daughter or the mother of your son does not depend on your will. These loves are dictated by nature. Instead,

5. Johann Wolfgang von Goethe, *Faust*, Part II: "Alles Vergängliche / ist nur ein Gleichnis."

the choice of this particular woman as your bride, or of this particular man as your husband, depends (or should depend!) only on your freedom. And God, who is freedom, wants a free love from his creatures.

39.
Faith, Hope, and Charity: The Triptych of Beauty

A famous theologian of the fifth or sixth century, once naively mistaken for the Dionysius who converted after Paul's discourse at the Areopagus in Athens (Acts 17:34)—wrote one of the loftiest praises of divine beauty:

> God is called Beautiful because It is All-Beautiful and more than Beautiful, and is eternally, unvaryingly, unchangeably Beautiful. . . . From this Beautiful all things possess their existence, each kind being beautiful in its own manner. . . . And by the Beautiful all things are united together and the Beautiful is the beginning of all things, as being the Creative Cause which moves the world and holds all things in existence by their yearning for their own Beauty. And It is the Goal of all things, and their Beloved, as being their Final Cause from which they derive their definite limits.[1]

This praise, however, has a serious defect. It deals with the *essential* beauty of God, not the *personal* one. The attribute of beauty expresses the relationship between God and creation, as the cause and transcendent model of all beauty. According to the Platonic vision of the author, the Beautiful and the One are the

---

1. Pseudo-Dionysius the Areopagite, *On the Divine Names*, IV, 7 (PG 3, 701–704) (trans. C.E. Rolt).

same. Beauty applies therefore to the divinity in general, not to the persons. It is a *divine*, but not a *Trinitarian*, beauty. (Beautiful [*kalòn*] is referred to as an "It," not as a "He" or "They"!)

If God, however, is beautiful, he must be such for someone who is co-eternal with him. Just as there is no music where there is no ear to hear it, so there is no beauty where there is no eye (physical or spiritual) to admire it. And for whom is God beautiful if he were not a Trinity of persons? For creatures? In that case he would be beautiful only since the world has existed, not to mention that no creature is able to reflect the divine beauty, which is infinite and transcendent.

The truth is that beauty is an attribute of the persons more than of their nature. Beautiful are the three divine persons! The Father is beautiful for the Son, as the Son is for the Father, who finds in him all his delight. The same must be said of the common Breath, which is the Spirit, even if for him there are no human categories with which to represent him, not even that of "person"; only images and symbols: the dove, the perfume, the dew, and the fire. The Trinity, we have said above, allows God to love himself without selfishness. We must add that the Trinity allows God to admire himself without narcissism.

Trinitarian beauty is a beauty made up of relationships, just as "pure relationships" are the very persons of the Trinity. The least inadequate images of this beauty are those of music and dance. In the musical accord, each note draws its beauty from the harmony it creates with the others; in choral dance, each movement draws beauty from coordination with the movement of others.

This is the beauty that Rublëv managed to represent in his famous icon of the Trinity. A beauty that emanates from the way each person relates to the other two—that is, from the harmony of their movements and the concentration of all gazes toward the center. Unity is expressed by their glances, diversity by the different color and distinct posture. It is a dynamic beauty, not a static one. Each of the three angels of the icon can be reproduced separately (as sometimes has been done), but the enchantment is broken and all the strength of the icon is lost.

Facing Rublëv's icon of the Trinity, it is natural to make a comparison with Botticelli's "Three Graces," already known to us. This should not sound blasphemous, for it is commonly accepted that Botticelli, a Platonist but also a pious Christian and a disciple of Savonarola, wanted to represent precisely three virtues (we do not know whether the theological ones or others). The same beauty we observe in the three divine persons of Rublëv's icon can be seen in the three graces of the Florentine painter. A beauty expressed by the harmony and the levity of their movements and the common pointing of their hands upward to the same direction.

But now let us go beyond what art can tell us about beauty. Leaving aside images and symbols, let us look for the reality. What do the three theological virtues have to do with beauty? Pascal said that there are three orders, or levels, of greatness in the world: the order of bodies and material things, the order of intelligence and genius, and the order of holiness. Strength, physical beauty, and material wealth belong to the first order; genius, science, and art belong to the second; goodness, holiness, and grace belong to the third. Between each one of these orders and the next, there is a leap in quality. The fact of being rich or poor, beautiful or ugly neither adds nor detracts anything from genius; its greatness is placed on a different and higher level. In the same way, the fact of being strong or weak, rich or poor, a genius or an illiterate neither adds nor detracts anything from the saints: their greatness is placed on a different and infinitely superior level.[2] Unlike the other two, this greatness does not depend on nature or fortune but on what is most noble in us humans, our freedom. And it lasts for eternity!

2. B. Pascal, *Pensées*, 793, ed. Brunschvicg.

Everything Pascal says about *greatness* in general must be said about *beauty*. There are three orders of beauty: the physical order or bodily beauty, the order of intellectual and artistic beauty, and the order of spiritual beauty. The third degree of beauty has a name that encompasses everything: grace. This word, which is synonymous in human language with beauty, attractiveness, and charm, is also the term that sums up the inner beauty of the soul. "God's better beauty, grace," wrote a poet.[3] Nothing in the world—wonder of nature or work of art—speaks to us so directly of divine beauty as grace does. Grace is not just a pale reflection of, but a direct participation in, that same beauty. St. Teresa of Avila who once saw the splendor of a soul in grace, compares it to a mirror that reflects light from all sides,[4] and St. Catherine of Siena says that "in this world there is nothing that can equal the beauty of a soul in grace."[5] God alone knows the spiritual beauty of his creature, being the only one who knows himself in whose image man and woman were created.

Now, what is "a soul in grace" if not the soul possessing faith, hope, and charity? All three theological virtues, together, contribute to spiritual beauty, but one of them more directly than the other two: their queen, charity. The words that Dostoevsky puts on the lips of one of his favorite characters, the Idiot, are well known: "The world will be saved by beauty." But to that statement a question is immediately added: "What beauty will save the world?"[6] It is clear that not every beauty will save the world. There is, in fact, a beauty that can save the world and a beauty that can ruin it. The writer himself, in a letter to his niece, tells us what he thinks is the beauty that can save the world: "There is

3. G.M. Hopkins, "To What Serves Mortal Beauty."
4. Teresa of Avila, *Life*, 40, 5.
5. Raymond of Capua, *Life of St. Catherina*, 151.
6. F. Dostoevsky, *The Idiot*, III, chap. 5.

only one absolutely beautiful being in the world, whose appearance is a miracle of beauty: Christ!"[7]

With regard to Christ, the contrast between two affirmations is striking. On the one hand, he is seen as "the fairest of the sons of men" (Ps 45:3), as "the radiance of divine glory" (Heb 1:3); on the other hand, the words once said of the Suffering Servant are applied to him in his Passion: "He had no majestic bearing to catch our eye, no beauty to draw us to him" (Is 53:2). The explanation of this contrast is simple: Jesus redeemed beauty by depriving himself of it out of love. Christ revealed that there is something greater than the love of beauty, and it is the beauty of love!

Modern man, someone said, "doubts the truth, resists the good, but is fascinated by the beautiful." The world keeps offering people beauty recipes, and I, too, want to offer one. It is not mine, but from my friend St. Augustine: "You become beautiful by loving God." An ugly man, he explains, does not become beautiful because he loves a beautiful woman. But what is impossible in the physical realm is possible in the spiritual. "Our soul is ugly because of sin; it becomes beautiful by loving God who is beauty itself. The more love grows in you, the more your beauty grows."[8] Man is what he loves!

Hopkins will forgive me for paraphrasing his famous verse in this way: "God's better beauty, love"!

7. F. Dostoevsky, Letter to Sonija Ivànova.

8. Augustine, *On the First Letter of John*, 9.

40.

Behold, I Stand at the Door and Knock

At the end of our entertainment with the three beautiful sisters, faith, hope, and charity, let us go back to the words of the Risen One from which we started:

> Behold, I stand at the door and knock.
> If anyone hears my voice and opens the door,
> I will enter his house and dine with him,
> and he with me. (Rv 3:20)

Exegetes are debating whether this text has an eschatological or a mystical meaning: that is, whether it refers to the final coming of Christ or to the interior one that is taking place here and now when we welcome the Lord in the liturgy and in our life. In other words, whether the supper that Jesus promises is that of the Lamb in the heavenly Jerusalem or that mystical and Eucharistic one on earth.

The biblical passages that resonate in that text lead to a mystical interpretation, in the sense of an encounter that takes place, right now, through love. One of these passages is Song of Songs 5:2: "The sound of my lover knocking! 'Open to me, my sister, my friend'"; another is John 14:23: "Whoever loves me will keep my word, and my Father will love him, and we will come to him and make our dwelling with him." It is therefore the bridegroom who speaks in that text of the Revelation, not the eschatological judge. The judge, too, "is at the gates" (Jas 5:9), but he does not knock and wait. Rather, he comes "as a thief in the night" (Mt 24:43). In the presence of the judge, we are not free to make the choice, as we are while on earth.

The English painter Holman Hunt (1827–1910), of the so-called Pre-Raphaelite school, in a famous painting entitled *The Light of the World*, was inspired by our verse from Revelation. In the Victorian era, his painting was the subject of a real devotion within the Anglican Church. It toured the English colonies and was then placed in St. Paul's Cathedral in London, where it can still be seen today. In the painting, Jesus, barefoot and with a lantern in his hand, stands in front of a door on which brambles and weeds have grown. He has just knocked and is waiting for a sign of an answer. During one of the exhibitions, someone from the audience pointed out to the painter—known for his meticulous attention to detail—that there was, however, a missing detail in his painting: "You forgot to put the handle on the door." And the painter replied: "Oh, no, this is done on purpose. There is only one handle on that door and it is inside." (I explained at the beginning how this answer should be understood.)

This "paschal" interpretation of Jesus knocking at the door (he appears crowned with thorns!) is not the only one existing; there is also a "Christmas" version of the same subject. In these naïve images, we see the baby Jesus barefoot, with snow around his feet, who at night, with a lantern in his hand, after knocking, is waiting in front of a door. The pagans imagined love as a child to whom they gave the name *Eros*. It was a symbolic representation, indeed an idol. We know that love has truly become a child, that it is now a reality, an event, indeed a person, the baby Jesus.

With the coming of Christ, the great and tumultuous river of human history has reached a "lock" and resumes its course at a higher level. "The old things have passed away; behold, new things have come" (2 Cor 5:17). The great "gap" that separated God from man, the Creator from the creature, is filled. This is why human history has since been divided into "before Christ" and "after Christ."

We—modern Magi *from the West*—have arrived at Bethlehem and we lay down our gifts before the Great King: faith, hope, and charity. With a heart filled with gratitude, let us join in the wonder and joy of the liturgy, which at Christmas repeats as an accomplished fact the words of Isaiah 9:5. Mentally accompanying the words with the jubilant melody of Händel's *Messiah*, let us proclaim:

> For unto us a Child is born,
> unto us a Son is given;
> and the Government shall be upon his Shoulder,
> and his Name shall be called
> Wonderful, Counselor,
> The Mighty God,
> The Everlasting Father,
> The Prince of Peace!

Excursus 1
Did Jesus Possess the
Theological Virtues?

On the sidelines of our reflections on the theological virtues, we ask the most delicate question about them: Did Jesus know and practice the three theological virtues: faith, hope, and charity?

One of the titles given to Jesus in the Litany of the Sacred Heart is "Heart of Jesus, abyss of all virtues."[1] Jesus practiced in a supreme way—divine and human—the four cardinal virtues: prudence, justice, fortitude, and temperance. (A single page of the Passion accounts contains more on them than all the lives of the saints put together.) He possessed, in a transcendent degree, all the moral virtues of the Bible: obedience, humility, meekness, and so on. Did he also practice the three theological virtues? We are entering a sacred space and must take the shoes off our feet—that is, remove every presumption from our mind. The question, however, is too important not to be asked. I believe the answer must be yes! In a different way and infinitely more perfect than ours, but he possessed them.

Let us start with faith. Many exegetes today believe that the expression "the faith of Christ" or "the faith of the Son of God," which occurs six times in the writings of Paul,[2] at least in some cases, does not indicate faith *in* Christ but the faith *of* Christ—that is, the fidelity he gave proof of in the voluntary

1. *Cor Jesu, virtutum omnium abyssus.*
2. Rom 3:22; 3:26; Gal 2:16; 2:20; 3:22; Phil 3:9.

sacrifice of himself on the cross.[3] If faith, as St. Paul teaches us, is fundamentally obedience to God and filial abandonment to him, no one has ever had a more perfect faith than Jesus. In this sense—subjective and not just objective—we can read the words of the Letter to the Hebrews that define Jesus as "the author and perfecter of faith"—that is, "he who gives rise to faith and brings it to completion" (Heb 12:2).

Can the same be said of hope? I think yes! Jesus did not die on the cross like someone who knows he has an ace up his sleeve that he will pull out at the right moment. He was not reciting a script, like someone who knows by heart what will come next! The Resurrection was for him, in a way that we cannot understand and define, an object of hope. The Apostle Peter, on the day of Pentecost, applied to Jesus, in his death, the words of the Psalm that, in the Septuagint version, said:

> My flesh, too, will dwell in hope,
> because you will not abandon my soul to the netherworld,
> nor will you suffer your holy one to see corruption.
> (Acts 2:26–27)

Regarding the third theological virtue, charity, it would be almost blasphemous to ask whether Jesus possessed it: "No one has greater love than this, to lay down one's life for one's friends" (Jn 15:13). It seems that Jesus went even beyond this, giving his life for his *enemies*. Indeed, "while we were still sinners Christ died for us" (Rom 5:8). There is no contradiction. He gave his life for his enemies considering them his friends, as he did with Judas in Gethsemane (Mt 26:50).

The question to ask is rather a different one and concerns all three theological virtues. They are called "infused" virtues, but by whom could the virtues of Christ be infused if he himself is God?

3. R.B. Hays, *The Faith of Jesus Christ*, Chico, CA, 1983.

The answer is: from the same one who is said to have "poured out charity into our hearts"—that is, the Holy Spirit (Rom 5:5)! For what purpose was the Holy Spirit "upon him" at the moment of his baptism in the Jordan and "anointed him"? Certainly not only to bring the good news to the poor (Lk 4:18) but for all of his messianic work as king, prophet, and priest! The Letter to the Hebrews affirms (a most precious statement!): "Christ . . . through the eternal Spirit offered himself unblemished to God" (Heb 9:14). It was therefore the Holy Spirit who moved the human will of Jesus to offer himself as a victim of atonement, which is the supreme act of his charity toward us. Jesus' prayer, too, was aroused in his human heart by the Holy Spirit (Lk 10:21).

It is not a question of two operations of the Holy Spirit, successive and independent, as if he had first acted in Jesus and later, similarly, in believers. The relationship between the two actions is not only temporal but also causal. In other words, the theological virtues of Jesus are not only a model but also the cause and source of ours. "From his fullness we have all received, grace in place of grace" (Jn 1:16). What Jesus says about the Paraclete's entire work also applies to the theological virtues: "He will take from what is mine and declare it to you" (Jn 16:14). This is demonstrated by the fact that the Holy Spirit puts in the heart of the believer the cry "*Abba*, Father!" (Gal 4:6; Rom 8:15). For himself, the Spirit could not, in fact, call God *Abba*, because he is not generated but only proceeds from the Father. He can do this because it is the Spirit of the Son who continues the prayer of the Head in the members of his Body.

I am not aware if any of the ancient Fathers ever faced the problem of the theological virtues in Jesus. Knowing their respective positions, however, we can say how they would have solved it, if they had been asked. In short, here are the answers they would have given to the question of whether or not Jesus possessed the theological virtues:

—The Nestorians: "Yes, of course!"

—The Monophysites: "No, absolutely not!"

—The Church, both of the East and of the West: "Yes, but . . ."

I will try to explain myself. The Nestorians believed that in Jesus, there was not only a perfect *humanity* but also a perfect *man* whom they called the man assumed (*assumptus homo*). An autonomous subject of action, therefore, capable not only of moral virtues—obedience, humility, patience, etc.—but also of the theological virtues of faith, hope, and charity. In doing so, however, they did not save the unity of the person of Christ as a divine person, not a human one.

The Monophysites, on the other hand, believed that in Jesus there was "only one nature" (*physis*), the divine one, even if "incarnate." Humanity turned out to be in Christ a quality, or a "way of being," of his divine nature rather than a true and proper complete human nature. As a uniquely divine subject, Jesus could not therefore possess the theological virtues that have God as their object: it would have been like believing in himself, hoping in himself, and loving himself.

The Church, at Chalcedon in 451, defined Jesus as one person—that of the eternal Son of God—but existing in two natures, each endowed with its own properties. We ask ourselves: Among the properties of his human nature, was there also that of a "free" human will? It took more than two centuries to respond with a firm yes to this question. At the Third Council of Constantinople (680–681), the Church condemned the Monothelite heresy, which admitted in Christ a single "operative energy"—that is, a single will, the divine one.

The explanation that St. Maximus the Confessor gave, on that occasion, of Christ's obedience in Gethsemane,[4] also applies to the theological virtues. At this level, obedience and faith are

4. Maximus the Confessor, *Opuscula theologica* (PG 91, 68).

practically the same thing. "Not what I want, but what you want" (Mk 14:36): the distinction between that "I" and that "you"— that is, between the human will of Jesus and the will that he has in common with the Father—creates the space for the exercise of the theological virtues, even if (I do not tire of repeating) in a different way from ours. That is why I have qualified the answer of the Church as a "yes, but." Christ—and he alone—is both subject and object of the theological virtues. Subject, because as a man he practiced them; object, because as God he is the term, together with the Father and the Holy Spirit, of our faith, hope, and charity.

The question about the theological virtues of Jesus can help us in giving an answer to a problem that never ceases to haunt theologians and exegetes: In his earthly existence, was Jesus aware of being God? The believer's response, even in this case, can only be a positive: "Yes, and from the very first moment of the Incarnation!" Thinking differently would mean admitting the absurdity that, following the Incarnation, the eternal Word of God lost consciousness of himself, that a void was created in the Trinity, like a parenthesis and a suspension. The Father would cease being Father and the Son being Son; the dialogue and relationship that give rise to the Trinity would cease. (Unless we believe that only a stunt double for the Word was incarnated!) The Church Fathers enclosed the mystery of the Incarnation in the motto "He remained what he was and became what he was not" (*Quod erat permansit, quod non erat assumpsit*).[5] He did not come out of the Trinity to enter the world. There is some analogy with the awareness of being a man that the Risen One now preserves in heaven. When Jesus says "I" in the Gospels, he is truly a man who expresses himself, a man who, like all human beings, had to become aware of himself thanks to the molding love of his mother and of Joseph. But this "I" is, in a direct line, the one that allows, from

5. Augustine, *In Ioh.*, 80, 2; Gregory Nazianzen, *Oratio theologica*, III, 19.

eternity, the Father to be Father; it is the I of the eternal Son, the second person of the Trinity.

It is clear that all these affirmations of ours on the theological virtues of Jesus and on his consciousness of being God are possible only if we accept the Church's dogma of the two natures that subsist in the one person of Christ "without confusion, and without mutation." This truth, however, is professed, at least in principle, by all Christian confessions. It is a fruit of the development of faith, guided by the Holy Spirit who, as Jesus himself promised, would lead the Church "to the full truth" about him.

The true mystery, absolutely impenetrable for us, is how the divine self-awareness of Jesus could be reconciled with his being a man, with all the human limitations that the Gospel itself does not hesitate to highlight. This constitutes the insurmountable limit of human intelligence, to be accepted with joy and humility, as we humbly accept the mystery, also impenetrable for us, of the relationship between grace and freedom.

Excursus 2
From God as Love to
the *Filioque*

Starting from the revealed truth that "God is love," we can hope to reach a full reconciliation between Eastern and Western theology on the problem of the *Filioque*—that is, on the way the Holy Spirit proceeds in the Trinity: whether from the Father alone, as the Greeks affirm, or from the Father *and the Son* (in Latin, *Filioque*) as we profess in our Western theology.

The agreement could consist in accepting—on the part of us Latins—the Trinitarian *scheme* of the Greeks that starts from the plurality of persons (and more precisely from the person of the Father) to arrive at the unity of nature, and—on the part of the Greeks—in accepting (or at least recognizing the legitimacy of) the *content* that the Latins assign to the divine nature—namely, love in its distinction of lover, beloved, and love itself. This explanation is no more than an image, of course, but certainly less exposed to the suspicion of subordinationism than other images sometimes used by the Fathers, such as "the sun, the splendor, the ray," or "the source, the river, the stream." It was received, at least in part, among the Greeks by St. Gregory Palamas, who, in the fourteenth century, personally knew the treatise on the Trinity of St. Augustine. He writes:

> The Spirit of the Most High Word is like the Father's ineffable love for his Word, generated in an ineffable way; love that this

same Word and beloved Son of the Father has, in turn, for the Father, insofar as he possesses the Spirit which together with him comes from the Father and who rests in him, insofar as he is connatural.[1]

Latin theologians would only need to change the expression "with him," into the expression "through him."[2] In this light, the procession of the Holy Spirit from the Father and the Son (or from the Father through the Son), that is, the *Filioque*—apart from its undue addition to the symbol of faith—should no longer appear as a "heresy," but rather as a consequence of the Trinitarian love. A question remains otherwise unanswered: What did the Father not perfectly express of himself in the generation of the Son, to require a second, or a parallel, operation—that is, the spiration of the Holy Spirit?

To the right concern of Orthodox theology to assign to the Holy Spirit not only a passive but also an active role within the Trinity, theologians try to respond today by saying that, if the Holy Spirit proceeds from the Father and the Son (*ex Patre Filioque*), the Son too is generated by the Father "in the Holy Spirit" or "in the anointing of the Spirit."

All this is not an abstract speculation to be left to professional theologians, but it is something that concerns us closely, a mystery that has its replica within every soul in grace. If—as St. John of the Cross explained to us above—what happens by nature in the Trinity happens by grace in the soul, then we must say that also in us the Father generates his Son "in the Holy Spirit." It is, in fact, through the work of the Holy Spirit that one is "reborn

1. Gregory Palamas, *Capita physica*, 36 (PG 150, 1145).

2. Gregory of Nyssa has both expressions: "through him and together with him" (*C. Eunomium*, I, 48). Other Greek Fathers have written that the Holy Spirit proceeds from the Father "through the Son," that he is "image of the Son" (Athanasius, *Ad Serap.*, I, 24; Cyril of Alexandria, *In Johann.*, XI, 10; John Damascenus, *De fide orth.*, I, 13); that he "proceeds from the Father and receives from the Son"; that he is the "ray" coming from the sun (the Father) through its splendor (the Son), or that he is the "stream" coming from the source (the Father), through the river (the Son).

from above" (Jn 3:5–7), and it is through him that we become sons in the Son:

> For you did not receive a spirit of slavery to fall back into fear, but you received a spirit of adoption, through which we cry, "Abba, Father!" The Spirit itself bears witness with our spirit that we are children of God. (Rom 8:15–16)

The reciprocity between the Son and the Holy Spirit that exists in the Trinity (the "theology") is reflected in all of Christ's earthly work (the "economy"). At Easter, Jesus sends the Spirit to the disciples; but before then, the Holy Spirit is sent upon him. In the Incarnation, he is conceived by the work of the Holy Spirit; in baptism, he is anointed with the Holy Spirit with a kind of earthly replica of his eternal anointing at the moment of his generation; in prayer, he shouts *Abba* in the Holy Spirit (Lk 10:21). On the day of Pentecost, Peter perfectly summarizes this mystery of the Spirit being received and given by Jesus: "Exalted at the right hand of God, he received the promise of the holy Spirit from the Father and poured it forth, as you both see and hear" (Acts 2:33).

Many theologians—Catholics, Protestants, and Orthodox[3]—are now moving in this direction, and this allows us to hope that we can soon leave behind us the diatribe that for over a millennium has only produced division and mutual accusations between East and West, to announce to the world that God is a communion of love and calls us all to unity in love.

The unfortunate estrangement and separation between the Christian East and the Christian West has deprived both of them of the necessary counterweight and corrective of the

---

3. On these recent developments, see what I have written in my book *Come, Creator Spirit: Meditations on the "Veni Creator,"* Liturgical Press, Collegeville, MN, 2008, chap. XXII. For the Orthodox perspective, see Olivier Clément, *Sources. Les mystiques chrétiens des origines,* Paris, 1982.

deficiencies—or excesses—of their theology and spirituality. May they start being again, at the occasion of the second millenary of the Redemption in 2033, what they used to be, at least in part, in the first millennium—that is, two lungs with one breath!

Index of Names
and Authors

189